The U.S. Constitution Explained for Every American

A Simple, Clause-by-Clause Guide to Understanding Your Rights, Freedoms, and the Framework of American Democracy

SILAS KINGSLEY

COPYRIGHT NOTICE

Welcome to a journey through the U.S. Constitution—a document that has shaped the very fabric of our nation. We're thrilled to share this exploration with you, and we hope it sparks a deeper understanding of the rights, freedoms, and principles that govern us all.

This book is dedicated to the timeless pursuit of knowledge and justice. Whether you are a student, a scholar, or simply a curious reader, we hope this work enriches your understanding and empowers you to engage with the Constitution in meaningful ways.

Thank you for embarking on this journey with us. Here's to learning, growing, and exploring the heart of American democracy together.

TABLE OF CONTENTS

Introduction

How to Use This Book and What You'll Gain
From It

This book begins with a simple idea: the Constitution is not meant to intimidate. It was written to be read, lived with, and returned to over time. You do not need special training to understand it. You only need a calm place to start and a guide that moves at a human pace.

Many people first encounter the Constitution in moments of confusion or tension. A news headline. A public debate. A question about rights or power. Too often, the explanations that follow feel rushed, argumentative, or technical. This book exists to offer something different. It slows things down. It creates space to understand the document without pressure, noise, or judgment.

Think of this book as an open door. You are not expected to arrive with certainty or prior knowledge. You are invited to step inside, settle in, and take the Constitution one piece at a time. Nothing here assumes expertise. Nothing here asks you to rush.

The book can be read from beginning to end, or opened whenever a specific question arises. Each part of the Constitution is explained in the order it appears, using the same gentle structure throughout. First, the original words. Then a clear explanation of what those words mean. Then why they were written, what they allow or limit, and how they touch ordinary life. The repetition of this pattern is intentional. It creates familiarity, and familiarity builds comfort.

There is no demand to memorize clauses or remember dates. Understanding grows naturally through exposure and clarity. Over time, the Constitution begins to feel less like a distant artifact and more like a knowable framework. Something that can be revisited without anxiety.

Throughout the book, care is taken to keep explanations grounded and steady. What the Constitution says is treated separately from how courts have interpreted it and from how people argue about it today. This separation matters. It allows space to think clearly, without being pulled toward a conclusion.

Examples are drawn from everyday situations, chosen for their familiarity and neutrality. They are meant to illuminate, not provoke. The goal is ease, not urgency.

By the final pages, the Constitution should feel less heavy and more approachable. Its structure should feel orderly. Its language should feel less foreign. Most importantly, there should be a sense of confidence in opening the document again when questions arise.

This book offers a quiet welcome into one of the most important texts in American life. It is meant to steady, not to persuade. To clarify, not to overwhelm. To remind you that understanding is possible, and that you are allowed to take your time.

Part I

What the Constitution Is—and What It Is Not

The United States Constitution is a framework. It is not a detailed instruction manual for daily life, and it is not a collection of moral slogans. Its purpose is to organize power, limit authority, and set the basic rules by which a national government operates. Everything else in American law grows from this foundation.

At its core, the Constitution creates a government of limited powers. It does not give the federal government authority over every aspect of life. Instead, it lists specific powers and places boundaries around how those powers can be used. Where power is not granted, it is withheld or left elsewhere. This design was intentional, shaped by fear of centralized authority and a desire to preserve individual liberty.

The Constitution is also not a promise that government will always act wisely or fairly. It does not prevent mistakes, abuse, or injustice on its own. What it does is create mechanisms for accountability. Elections, separation of powers, judicial review, and amendments exist because the framers assumed imperfection, not because they expected ideal behavior.

It is important to understand what the Constitution does not do. It does not settle every political disagreement. It does not provide clear answers to every modern problem. It does not guarantee comfort, agreement, or ease. Many debates exist precisely because the Constitution leaves room for interpretation and change.

The Constitution is also not a static historical artifact. While its text is fixed unless amended, its application has evolved over time through court decisions, legislation, and social change. That evolution is part of the system, not a failure of it. At the same time, not everything can be changed simply because circumstances shift. The document balances flexibility with restraint.

Finally, the Constitution is not owned by any political party, generation, or institution. Its authority comes from the people as a whole. It belongs to everyone, and understanding it is not reserved for specialists. It was written to be read, argued over, and applied in public life.

How to Read Constitutional Language Without a Law Degree

Constitutional language can feel unfamiliar at first. The words are old, the sentences are formal, and the structure is different from modern writing. But the language follows rules, and once those rules are understood, the text becomes far more approachable.

The Constitution is organized in layers. Articles establish broad areas of government responsibility. Sections divide those responsibilities into specific functions. Clauses narrow those functions further by explaining how power works or where limits apply. Amendments modify or add to the original text without erasing it. Reading with this structure in mind prevents confusion and keeps each part in its proper place.

Clauses are the smallest working units of the Constitution. Each clause usually does one thing. It grants a power, places a restriction, defines a process, or protects a right. Reading clause by clause keeps the meaning contained and prevents assumptions from spreading beyond the text.

Understanding the difference between powers, rights, and limits is essential. Powers describe what government is allowed to do. Rights describe what individuals are protected from government interference. Limits describe what government is forbidden from doing, even when exercising its powers. Confusing these categories leads to misunderstanding and unnecessary conflict.

The Constitution also relies heavily on contrast. When power is given in one place and restricted in another, both matter equally. What is said and what is withheld work together. Silence in the Constitution is often intentional, not accidental.

Federal and state authority is another key distinction. The Constitution creates a national government with defined powers while preserving broad authority for the states. This division is known as federalism. It allows different levels of government to operate independently while remaining connected. Many constitutional disputes arise from disagreement over where one level of authority ends and another begins.

Words like "shall," "may," and "shall not" carry real weight. They signal obligation, permission, or prohibition. Reading carefully, without rushing, is often enough to clarify meaning without needing technical interpretation.

The Clause-by-Clause Method Used in This Book

This book uses a consistent method to reduce confusion and build understanding gradually. Each clause is treated as a complete idea before moving on to the next. Nothing is skipped, summarized loosely, or folded into general commentary.

Every clause begins with the original constitutional text. This is the anchor. The explanation that follows never replaces the text or asks you to ignore it. Instead, it works alongside it.

Next comes a plain-language explanation of what the clause is saying. This translation avoids legal terminology whenever possible and focuses on meaning rather than form. The goal is clarity, not simplification at the cost of accuracy.

Each clause is then placed in context. Why it was written matters. Many clauses were responses to specific problems, fears, or failures. Understanding those motivations helps explain why the language is structured the way it is.

After that, the practical effect of the clause is explained. What does it allow? What does it restrict? Who does it apply to? These questions ground the text in real life without drifting into opinion.

Where court interpretations are important, they are introduced carefully and briefly. The focus remains on what the Constitution says, not on turning the explanation into a legal debate. When disagreement exists, it is acknowledged calmly.

This method is repeated throughout the book. The repetition is deliberate. Familiar structure creates ease. Ease creates confidence. Confidence makes the Constitution something that can be returned to, not avoided.

This approach is meant to steady the experience of learning. It removes the pressure to keep up or already know the answers. Understanding is allowed to unfold naturally, one clause at a time.

Part II

The Failure of the Articles of Confederation

The Constitution did not appear out of confidence. It emerged out of strain, frustration, and hard experience. Before it existed, the young United States was governed by the Articles of Confederation, a document shaped almost entirely by fear of concentrated power.

The Articles reflected the mindset of a people who had just escaped a distant authority they believed had overreached. The priority was independence for the states, not strength for the nation. As a result, the national government created under the Articles was intentionally weak.

There was no executive branch. No single authority existed to carry out laws or respond decisively to national problems. There was no national court system to interpret disputes between states or ensure consistent application of law. Congress was the only national institution, and even its authority was narrow.

Congress could declare war, negotiate treaties, and manage foreign relations in theory. In practice, it struggled to do even these things effectively. It had no power to tax. It relied on states to voluntarily contribute money. When states refused or delayed, the national government simply went without. Soldiers went unpaid. Debts went unsettled. Confidence eroded.

Economic instability became a serious problem. States issued their own currencies, imposed tariffs on one another, and competed instead of cooperating. Interstate trade suffered. Foreign nations took advantage of the lack of coordination. The United States appeared fragmented and unreliable on the world stage.

Amending the Articles required unanimous consent from all thirteen states. This made reform nearly impossible. Even widely recognized problems remained unsolved because one state could block change. The system was locked in place, unable to adapt.

The weakness of the national government became painfully clear during moments of crisis. Shays' Rebellion, sparked by economic hardship and debt, exposed the government's inability to maintain order or respond collectively. The national government had no standing army and no authority to intervene effectively.

The failure of the Articles was not due to ignorance or lack of principle. It was the result of overcorrection. In trying to avoid tyranny, the system created paralysis. Independence without coordination proved unsustainable.

The lesson was unavoidable. A nation could not survive on shared ideals alone. It needed structure, authority, and balance. The Constitution was the response to that realization.

The Constitutional Convention and the Major Compromises

The Constitutional Convention of 1787 was called to address the weaknesses of the Articles of Confederation. What began as a meeting to revise an existing system quickly became something more ambitious. Delegates recognized that small adjustments would not be enough. The structure itself had to change.

The gathering brought together individuals with different experiences, priorities, and concerns. Some represented large, populous states. Others came from smaller states wary of being overshadowed. Some wanted a strong national government. Others feared replacing one form of dominance with another. Agreement was not assumed. It had to be built.

Representation was one of the earliest and most contentious issues. Larger states argued that representation should reflect population. Smaller states argued that equal state representation was necessary to preserve their influence. The compromise created two legislative chambers. One would represent the people proportionally. The other would represent the states equally. This solution balanced population-based power with state equality and remains central to the Constitution's design.

Slavery posed another profound and morally fraught challenge. While deeply unjust, it was woven into the economic and political realities of the time. Compromises over representation, taxation, and the continuation of the slave trade allowed the Constitution to move forward, but at a heavy cost. These compromises did not resolve the issue. They postponed it, embedding conflict into the document that would later require amendment and struggle to correct.

Executive power was approached with caution. The delegates wanted leadership capable of action, but not unchecked authority. The presidency was created with defined powers, balanced by legislative oversight and judicial review. Elections, term limits, and impeachment were built into the system to prevent abuse.

Federalism itself was a compromise. Authority was divided between national and state governments rather than concentrated in one place. This structure allowed for unity while preserving local control. It accepted that power could be shared without being weakened.

The convention was conducted in secrecy, not to exclude the public, but to allow honest debate without pressure. Disagreements were frequent. The final document was not seen as flawless. It was seen as workable.

The Constitution exists because compromise replaced rigidity. It was shaped by the recognition that disagreement is permanent and that systems must account for human imperfection. The structure that emerged was designed not to eliminate conflict, but to manage it peacefully over time.

That understanding is embedded in every article and clause that follows.

Federalists, Anti-Federalists, and the Demand for a Bill of Rights

When the Constitution was completed and sent to the states for ratification, agreement was far from guaranteed. The debates that followed were not minor disagreements over wording. They were deep concerns about power, liberty, and the future of self-government. Out of those debates emerged two broad perspectives that shaped the Constitution as it exists today.

Those who supported the new Constitution became known as Federalists. They believed the existing system under the Articles of Confederation had failed and that a stronger national government was necessary to preserve the union. Their support was rooted in practicality. They saw economic instability, foreign vulnerability, and internal disorder as signs that the nation needed firmer structure.

Federalists argued that the Constitution already protected liberty through its design. Power was divided among three branches. Authority was split between national and state governments. No single institution could act alone for long. In their view, this structure itself was the primary safeguard against tyranny.

Opposing this view were the Anti-Federalists. Their concern was not disorder, but overreach. They feared that a powerful national government, even one with limits, would eventually erode local control and individual freedom. To them, the Constitution resembled the distant authority they had recently fought to escape.

Anti-Federalists focused on what the Constitution lacked. It did not explicitly protect freedoms such as speech, religion, and the right to a fair trial. While Federalists believed these rights were implied or protected by structure, Anti-Federalists wanted them stated plainly. They did not trust implication where liberty was concerned.

The debate played out through public essays, letters, and town meetings. The Federalist Papers defended the Constitution's design, explaining how its mechanisms restrained power. Anti-Federalist writings warned that unchecked authority, even if well intentioned, could drift toward abuse.

The demand for a bill of rights became the turning point. Several states agreed to ratify the Constitution only with the understanding that amendments protecting individual liberties would follow. This was not an afterthought. It was a condition of trust.

The eventual agreement reflected the Constitution's deeper logic. Structure and explicit rights would work together. Power would be divided and restrained, and certain freedoms would be placed beyond ordinary government reach. The Bill of Rights was the bridge between these views.

How Amendments Changed the Original Design

The Constitution was never presented as unchangeable. Its framers understood that no generation could foresee every challenge or injustice that might arise. For that reason, a method for amendment was built directly into the document.

The amendment process was designed to be difficult, but not impossible. Change requires broad agreement across states and institutions. This ensures stability while allowing growth. Amendments reflect moments when consensus forms around the need for correction or expansion.

The first ten amendments, known as the Bill of Rights, changed the original design by making individual liberties explicit. They placed clear limits on federal power and clarified protections that many believed were essential to freedom.

Later amendments reshaped the Constitution more dramatically. The abolition of slavery, the definition of citizenship, and the guarantee of equal protection altered the moral and legal foundation of the nation. These changes did not merely adjust the system. They rebuilt it in crucial ways.

Other amendments expanded democratic participation. Voting rights were extended, elections were restructured, and representation was made more direct. These changes reflected a growing belief that legitimacy flows from broader inclusion.

Some amendments corrected structural problems. Presidential succession was clarified. Term limits were imposed. Outdated policies were reversed. These changes show the Constitution's capacity for self-correction.

Amendments do not replace the original document. They exist alongside it. Each amendment adds a layer of meaning without erasing what came before. The Constitution becomes richer and more complete through this process.

The ability to amend is one of the Constitution's greatest strengths. It acknowledges imperfection without surrendering stability. It allows the framework of American democracy to adapt while remaining anchored to its original purpose.

Part III

The Preamble

The Preamble is the opening statement of the Constitution, and though it does not carry the force of law, it is the heart and guiding purpose of the entire document. It lays out the foundational principles behind the Constitution and introduces the core values that would inform the structure of the new government.

"We the People" and Popular Sovereignty

The Preamble begins with the powerful phrase: **"We the People."** This opening is not just a formality—it establishes one of the most important concepts in the Constitution: **popular sovereignty**. This means that the authority of the government comes not from kings, monarchs, or even the states, but directly from the people themselves. It is the people who are the ultimate source of power, and this idea marked a radical shift in thinking from the monarchical systems that were common at the time.

By starting the Constitution with "We the People," the framers made it clear that the government was created to serve and reflect the will of the citizens. This is not just a ceremonial phrase; it's a foundational principle. Every law, policy, and decision made by the government flows from the consent of the governed, emphasizing that the government is accountable to the people, and that power is shared between the people and the institutions they create.

The Six Stated Purposes of the Constitution

After establishing that the people hold the power, the Preamble sets out the six key purposes for which the Constitution was created. These are broad goals, not detailed mandates, but they provide a clear framework for understanding why the Constitution exists and what it seeks to achieve.

1. To Form a More Perfect Union

The first purpose is to "form a more perfect Union." The word "perfect" here doesn't imply flawless or without fault but suggests that the new system is meant to be an improvement over the existing system under the Articles of Confederation. The Articles had created a loose confederation of states, but the lack of strong central authority had led to disorder, economic instability, and an inability to defend the nation as a whole. The Constitution was meant to create a stronger bond between states, ensuring that the nation could act in a unified way when needed.

The phrase reflects a recognition that while the Articles had their strengths, they were not sufficient to manage the growing needs of a country that was expanding in both size and complexity. A "more perfect Union" was necessary to keep the country together, particularly in moments of crisis or conflict.

2. To Establish Justice

The second stated purpose is to "establish Justice." Justice in this context refers to a legal system that treats all citizens equally and provides fair resolutions to disputes. Under the Articles of Confederation, the lack of a national court system meant that disputes between states, or between citizens and the government, often went unresolved or were inconsistently handled. The Constitution created a judicial system to enforce laws and protect rights, ensuring that justice was not left to the whims of individual states or local authorities.

The inclusion of "justice" highlights the idea that law should be applied equally, fairly, and without bias, and that the courts would play a central role in preserving this equality across the nation.

3. To Insure Domestic Tranquility

The third purpose is to "insure domestic Tranquility." This refers to the idea of maintaining peace and order within the country. The framers were deeply aware of the need for stability and security, especially after experiencing events like Shays' Rebellion, which demonstrated how unrest and economic hardship could undermine the country's stability. The Constitution created a government with the power to respond effectively to internal threats, ensuring that the government could maintain public order and manage civil disturbances when necessary.

While it does not mean the government would have unchecked power over citizens, it ensures that the government had the authority to address and manage crises that could threaten peace within the country.

4. To Provide for the Common Defense

The fourth purpose is to "provide for the common defense." The Constitution created a national military to defend the nation against external threats. The framers understood that security was one of the government's most fundamental responsibilities. Unlike under the Articles of Confederation, where states were largely responsible for their own defense, the Constitution centralized military power to ensure a unified defense against foreign enemies.

This power allows the government to maintain and fund armed forces, declare war (with Congress's approval), and provide for the protection of the nation's sovereignty and territorial integrity.

5. To Promote the General Welfare

The fifth purpose is to "promote the general Welfare." This phrase is one of the most debated in the Constitution because it suggests that the government has the power to act in the best interests of the nation as a whole. Some argue that this grants broad authority for economic regulation and social welfare programs, while others believe it is more limited, referring to maintaining conditions that allow the country to flourish—like regulating interstate commerce, providing for national defense, and ensuring basic infrastructure.

Ultimately, the intent behind this clause was to allow the government to act in a way that benefits the nation, particularly in times of crisis, but within the limits of the other powers outlined in the Constitution.

6. To Secure the Blessings of Liberty to Ourselves and Our Posterity

The final purpose is to "secure the Blessings of Liberty to ourselves and our Posterity." This phrase emphasizes that the Constitution is not just about creating a stable government but also about protecting the freedoms and rights of future generations. It acknowledges that liberty is something that must be actively preserved and protected. The phrase "our Posterity" is important—it stresses that the framers did not just act for their own time but for future generations who would live under the Constitution's framework.

The Preamble sets up a government whose central goal is to protect individual freedoms while balancing that with the needs of the nation as a whole. This statement links the Constitution directly with the ideals of liberty, freedom, and the pursuit of happiness.

The Preamble, in these six purposes, establishes the overarching goals of the Constitution. It creates a government of the people, by the people, and for the people, with the main goal of preserving liberty and justice. It lays the groundwork for the federal system that follows and offers an enduring vision of what the United States is meant to be—a union of states and people working together for the common good, bound by the shared ideals of liberty, justice, and mutual respect.

Article I: The Legislative Branch

Article I of the U.S. Constitution establishes the legislative branch, which is responsible for making the laws of the nation. The framers of the Constitution gave Congress significant powers because they saw a strong, representative legislature as key to ensuring the government remained accountable to the people. Article I outlines the structure, powers, and functions of the legislative branch, detailing its two chambers: the House of Representatives and the Senate.

Section 1: Legislative Power Vested in Congress

The first section of Article I grants all legislative power to **Congress**, which consists of two chambers: the **House of Representatives** and the **Senate**. This section makes clear that the responsibility to create and pass laws does not lie with the president or the courts, but solely with the legislative branch.

By vesting this power in Congress, the framers created a body that would be directly accountable to the people (through the House) and to the states (through the Senate). It sets up the basic structure of the U.S. government: the president enforces the law, the courts interpret the law, and Congress makes the law.

Section 2: The House of Representatives

Section 2 focuses on the **House of Representatives**. It outlines the composition, qualifications, and powers of this chamber.

- **Composition**: The House is designed to represent the people directly. Each state is allotted a number of representatives based on its population, ensuring that larger states have more influence in the House than smaller ones. However, all states, regardless of size, are guaranteed at least one representative.

- **Qualifications**: To serve in the House, a representative must be at least **25 years old**, have been a citizen of the U.S. for at least **seven years**, and must be a resident of the state they represent at the time of election.

- **Elections**: Representatives serve **two-year terms**, and elections are held every even-numbered year. This short term ensures that House members remain responsive to their constituents and are frequently held accountable at the polls.

- **The Speaker of the House**: The House is presided over by the **Speaker**, who is elected by its members. The Speaker has significant authority over the legislative process, including deciding which bills are brought to the floor for debate and vote.

Section 3: The Senate

Section 3 establishes the **Senate**, the second chamber of Congress. The Senate was designed to be a more stable, deliberative body, balancing the immediate responsiveness of the House with a longer-term perspective.

- **Composition**: The Senate consists of **two senators** from each state, regardless of its population size.

This was a compromise to ensure that smaller states had an equal voice in the federal government.

- **Qualifications**: Senators must be at least **30 years old**, have been a U.S. citizen for at least **nine years**, and must be a resident of the state they represent.

- **Elections**: Senators serve **six-year terms**, with one-third of the Senate up for election every two years. This creates stability, as only a portion of the Senate is up for election at any given time.

- **The Vice President**: The **Vice President** of the United States serves as the **President of the Senate**. However, the Vice President's role is largely ceremonial, with the real work of presiding over the Senate handled by a **President Pro Tempore**, a senior member chosen by the Senate.

- **Impeachment Trials**: The Senate also holds the power to try impeachment cases. If the House of Representatives impeaches a federal official (including the president), the Senate holds the trial. Conviction requires a two-thirds majority vote.

Section 4: Elections and Sessions

Section 4 grants states the authority to regulate the times, places, and manner of holding elections for Senators and Representatives, but Congress has the power to alter those regulations if it chooses to.

- **Elections**: While the states initially had the authority to determine how elections would be held, Congress can make changes if needed. This power helps ensure that federal elections are consistent across states, maintaining fairness and order.

- **Sessions**: Congress must meet at least once every year, with the meeting occurring on the first Monday in December unless they decide otherwise. The section ensures that Congress is regularly convened to carry out its work, but also provides flexibility to adjust the schedule if necessary.

Section 5: Rules and Discipline

Section 5 grants each chamber of Congress—**the House of Representatives** and **the Senate**—the power to set its own rules, judge the qualifications of its members, and discipline members as needed.

- **Rules**: Each chamber has the authority to create its own rules for how it operates, including procedures for how bills are debated and voted on.

- **Expulsion and Censure**: If a member of either chamber is found guilty of misconduct, that chamber can expel them by a two-thirds vote, or censure them (a formal reprimand) by a majority vote.

Section 6: Pay, Privileges, and Conflicts

Section 6 discusses the pay, privileges, and limitations of members of Congress.

- **Compensation**: Senators and Representatives are paid for their service from the U.S. Treasury. The exact amount is set by law, and it has evolved over time. The section ensures that lawmakers are compensated for their time and efforts in public service.

- **Privileges**: Members of Congress are granted certain privileges to help them perform their duties, such as the **Freedom of Speech** in the course of legislative debate. This protection ensures that legislators can speak freely without fear of being sued or arrested.

- **Conflicts of Interest**: Members of Congress are forbidden from holding any office in the executive branch while serving in Congress. This rule prevents conflicts of interest and ensures that legislators focus on their legislative duties.

Section 7: How Laws Are Made

Section 7 lays out the process by which a bill becomes law.

- **Introducing Bills**: A bill can be introduced in either the House or the Senate, but if it involves raising revenue, it must originate in the House of Representatives.

- **Approval**: After a bill is introduced, it goes through a series of stages, including committee review, debate, and amendments. Both chambers must approve the bill in the same form before it can be sent to the president.

- **Presidential Action**: If Congress passes a bill, the president can either sign it into law or veto it. If the president vetoes a bill, Congress can override the veto with a two-thirds majority vote in both chambers. If the president does not act within ten days, the bill automatically becomes law unless Congress has adjourned.

Section 8: Enumerated Powers of Congress

Section 8 lists the specific powers granted to Congress. These powers are the heart of legislative authority and allow Congress to create laws on a broad range of topics. Some key powers include:

- **Taxation**: The power to levy taxes and provide for the common defense and general welfare.

- **Regulation of Commerce**: The authority to regulate interstate and foreign trade.

- **War Powers**: The power to declare war, raise and support armies, and provide for a navy.

- **Money and Counterfeiting**: The authority to coin money, regulate its value, and punish counterfeiting.

- **Immigration and Bankruptcy**: The power to establish laws on naturalization (immigration) and bankruptcy.

These enumerated powers give Congress the ability to legislate on many aspects of national governance, from economic policy to military matters, ensuring the functioning of a national government.

Section 9: Limits on Congress

Section 9 places certain limits on the powers of Congress to protect individual liberties and prevent governmental overreach. These limitations include:

- **Writ of Habeas Corpus**: The right to a writ of habeas corpus—ensuring that individuals cannot be unlawfully detained without being informed of charges against them.

- **Bills of Attainder and Ex Post Facto Laws**: Congress is prohibited from passing laws that punish individuals without trial (bills of attainder) or laws that make an act criminal after the fact (ex post facto laws).

- **Taxing Exports**: Congress is prohibited from taxing exports from any state.

- **Titles of Nobility**: Congress is forbidden from granting titles of nobility or accepting gifts from foreign governments.

These limits help preserve the balance of power and safeguard the rights of individuals against potential abuses of power.

Section 10: Limits on the States

Section 10 lists specific actions that states are forbidden from taking. These limitations ensure that the national government maintains authority over matters of national concern and that no state acts in a way that would disrupt national unity. Among the prohibitions are:

- **Foreign Affairs**: States cannot enter into treaties, alliances, or confederations with foreign nations.

- **Coining Money**: States are prohibited from coining their own money or issuing paper currency.

- **Imposing Tariffs**: States cannot impose duties or taxes on imports or exports without the consent of Congress.

- **War and Defense**: States cannot declare war or maintain standing armies or navies during peacetime.

These restrictions were designed to preserve the authority of the federal government and prevent states from acting in ways that could undermine national unity.

Article II: The Executive Branch

Article II of the U.S. Constitution establishes the executive branch of the federal government, with the president at its head. This article defines the powers, duties, and responsibilities of the president, as well as the process for presidential elections and impeachment. The goal of this article is to ensure that the executive branch is capable of carrying out the will of the people and implementing laws passed by Congress while balancing the power of the legislative and judicial branches.

Section 1: The Presidency and Elections

Section 1 begins by establishing the presidency and the process by which the president is elected. It specifies the **term** of the president (four years), and outlines the election process, including the role of the **Electoral College**.

- **Vesting of executive power**: The president holds the executive power of the United States, meaning the president is responsible for enforcing laws, directing the operations of the federal government, and ensuring national security.

- **Electoral College**: The president is not directly elected by a popular vote, but rather by the **Electoral College**, which consists of electors from each state. Each state is allocated a number of electors equal to its total number of senators and representatives in Congress. The system was designed as a compromise between those who wanted the president elected by popular vote and those who wanted Congress to elect the president.

- **Qualifications**: The president must meet certain qualifications: at least **35 years old**, a **natural-born citizen** of the U.S., and have lived in the U.S. for at least **14 years**.

- **Election process**: Presidential elections are held every **four years** on the first Tuesday after the first Monday in November. Voters cast ballots for electors, who then vote to elect the president and vice president. If no candidate receives a majority of the electoral votes, the decision is made by the **House of Representatives**.

- **Presidential succession**: The section also includes provisions for what happens if the president is unable to perform their duties, specifically outlining the role of the **vice president** in such cases and the procedure for presidential succession.

Section 2: Presidential Powers

Section 2 outlines the specific powers granted to the president. These powers are meant to allow the president to carry out the responsibilities of the office while maintaining checks on their authority.

- **Commander-in-chief**: The president is the commander-in-chief of the armed forces, including the Army, Navy, and Air Force. This role gives the president significant authority over military decisions, though Congress retains the power to declare war and provide military funding.

- **Treaties and foreign relations**: The president has the power to make treaties with foreign nations, but those treaties must be approved by a two-thirds majority of the **Senate**.

- **Appointments**: The president can appoint federal officers, including **cabinet members**, **judges**, and **ambassadors**, with the advice and consent of the Senate. This power allows the president to shape the administration and the judicial branch of the federal government.

- **Pardons**: The president has the power to grant pardons and reprieves for federal crimes, except in cases of impeachment. This power allows the president to forgive or reduce the penalties for individuals convicted of federal offenses.

- **State of the Union**: The president is required to provide a **State of the Union** address to Congress from time to time. This address allows the president to communicate the administration's priorities, outline legislative proposals, and set the policy agenda for the coming year.

Section 3: Presidential Duties

Section 3 outlines the duties and responsibilities of the president in relation to both the legislative and executive branches of government.

- **State of the Union**: As mentioned in Section 2, the president is required to periodically address Congress on the state of the nation. This address is an opportunity for the president to inform Congress of important matters and offer policy recommendations.

- **Enforcing laws**: The president is tasked with ensuring that the laws passed by Congress are faithfully executed. This responsibility gives the president significant influence over how laws are interpreted and implemented across the nation.

- **Calling special sessions**: The president has the authority to call Congress into **special session** if urgent matters arise that require immediate attention. This ensures that the government can act quickly in times of crisis.

- **Receiving foreign ambassadors**: The president serves as the official representative of the U.S. in foreign relations, and has the power to receive and interact with foreign diplomats, ambassadors, and heads of state.

- **Ensuring laws are executed**: The president must ensure that federal laws are enforced and that all executive departments and agencies carry out the policies set forth by Congress and the executive branch.

Section 4: Impeachment

Section 4 outlines the procedures for **impeachment**, the process by which a president (or any federal official) can be removed from office for committing "high crimes and misdemeanors."

- **Grounds for impeachment**: The president, vice president, and all civil officers of the United States are subject to impeachment for committing high crimes and misdemeanors. This provision ensures that no president, no matter how powerful, is above the law.

- **Impeachment process**: Impeachment begins in the **House of Representatives**, where articles of impeachment are drawn up and voted on. If a majority of the House votes in favor of impeachment, the case is then sent to the **Senate** for a trial.

- **Senate trial**: The Senate conducts the trial and has the authority to convict and remove the president from office. Conviction requires a two-thirds majority vote in the Senate. If the president is convicted, they are removed from office, and the vice president becomes president.

- **Punishments**: Impeachment does not necessarily result in criminal penalties, but it does remove the official from office. The individual may still face criminal charges in a court of law, separate from the impeachment process.

Article II grants significant powers to the presidency while also placing checks and balances on that power. It defines the president's role as the leader of the executive branch, the commander-in-chief of the military, and the figurehead of U.S. foreign policy. By clearly outlining the powers, duties, and limitations of the executive branch, the Constitution ensures that the president has the authority to govern while preventing any one individual from accumulating unchecked power.

Article III: The Judicial Branch

Article III of the U.S. Constitution establishes the judicial branch of the federal government. This branch is responsible for interpreting the laws and ensuring that they are applied fairly. It gives the judiciary the power to resolve disputes, clarify the meaning of laws, and check the actions of the legislative and executive branches, ensuring that the government adheres to the Constitution. The judicial branch operates independently, ensuring that laws are not only passed and enforced, but also interpreted correctly.

Section 1: The Federal Courts

Section 1 of Article III creates the structure of the federal judiciary and provides important details about the independence and authority of the courts.

- **Establishment of courts**: The Constitution establishes the **Supreme Court** as the highest court in the land, and grants Congress the power to create and organize lower federal courts as necessary. These lower courts would handle the bulk of cases involving federal law, with the Supreme Court acting as the final arbiter for appeals and constitutional questions.

- **Judicial independence**: The section ensures the independence of the judiciary by granting federal judges **life tenure**, meaning they serve "during good behavior." This lifetime appointment helps insulate judges from political pressure and ensures that they can make decisions based on the law and their interpretations of the Constitution, rather than fear of losing their position.

- **Compensation**: The salaries of federal judges cannot be reduced during their time in office, which further secures their independence. By guaranteeing financial stability, the Constitution helps prevent the executive or legislative branches from using financial pressure to influence judicial decisions.

- **Impartiality**: The Constitution's protections ensure that the judicial branch remains impartial and free from outside influence, allowing judges to uphold the rule of law even in politically sensitive cases. The provision of life tenure allows judges to make decisions that may not always be popular or politically convenient, but which are rooted in law.

Section 2: Judicial Power and Jurisdiction

Section 2 defines the scope and limits of the judicial power, setting clear boundaries on the cases and issues that the courts can hear.

- **Judicial power**: The judicial branch is vested with the power to resolve disputes arising under the Constitution, federal laws, and treaties. This power is essential for upholding the rule of law and ensuring that federal laws are interpreted consistently across all states.

- **Jurisdiction**: This section also sets forth the jurisdiction (or authority) of federal courts. Federal courts have jurisdiction over cases involving:

- o Federal laws and treaties

- o Disputes between two or more states

- o Cases involving the federal government as a party

- o Cases involving citizens of different states (diversity jurisdiction) when the amount in controversy exceeds a specified amount

- o Cases involving admiralty and maritime law

The concept of jurisdiction limits what federal courts can hear, ensuring that courts focus on issues related to federal law or disputes that require national resolution, rather than local or state issues that are better handled by state courts.

- **Supreme Court's original and appellate jurisdiction**: Section 2 specifies that the **Supreme Court** has original jurisdiction in cases involving ambassadors, public ministers, and consuls, as well as cases where a state is a party. In all other cases, the Supreme Court has appellate jurisdiction, meaning it can hear cases that have already been decided by lower courts. The structure ensures that the highest court in the land can step in when necessary but generally leaves the bulk of judicial work to lower courts.

- **Trial by jury**: This section guarantees the right to trial by jury in criminal cases. This protection is a critical safeguard of individual rights, ensuring that individuals accused of crimes will be judged by a jury of their peers, which provides fairness and prevents bias.

Section 3: Treason

Section 3 defines **treason** against the United States and establishes the procedures for prosecution and conviction. This section is important because it limits the power of the government to accuse individuals of treason and ensures that such accusations are made under strict legal standards.

- **Definition of treason**: Treason is defined as levying war against the United States, or adhering to its enemies, giving them aid and comfort. This narrow definition prevents overreach and ensures that accusations of treason are limited to acts that directly threaten the nation's security. The framers wanted to ensure that accusations of treason would not be used for political purposes or to silence political opposition.

- **Conviction requirements**: To be convicted of treason, there must be **two witnesses** to the same overt act of treason, or the individual must confess in open court. This high standard of evidence was deliberately included to prevent false or politically motivated charges, ensuring that the punishment for treason—being sentenced to death—would not be used recklessly.

- **Punishment for treason**: The punishment for treason can be severe, but the Constitution allows the punishment to be determined by Congress. However, it also includes a significant safeguard: the punishment for treason cannot extend to the family of the accused. This means that children or other relatives cannot be punished for the actions of someone convicted of treason, which prevents families from being punished collectively for the actions of one individual.

Article III establishes the judiciary as a vital, independent branch of the federal government. It ensures that the courts have the authority and structure needed to interpret the law and resolve disputes, protecting both the Constitution and the individual rights of citizens. By providing for judicial independence, limiting the scope of treason accusations, and setting strict standards for cases involving the federal government, Article III plays a critical role in the system of checks and balances. This article ensures that the judicial branch can serve as an impartial arbiter in disputes, maintaining the balance of power between the branches and safeguarding the rights of the people.

Article IV: The States and the Union

Article IV of the U.S. Constitution outlines the relationship between the states and the federal government, as well as the relationship between individual states themselves. It aims to create a balance between state sovereignty and federal authority, ensuring that states cooperate with each other while also providing for federal oversight and protection when necessary. This article addresses the powers and responsibilities of states, the movement of citizens between states, and the creation of new states, among other key topics.

Full Faith and Credit

Section 1 of Article IV addresses the principle of **full faith and credit** between states. This clause requires states to recognize and honor the public acts, records, and judicial proceedings of every other state. Essentially, it ensures that legal decisions and public records are respected across state lines, promoting consistency and cooperation among the states.

- **Legal Precedent**: A court decision made in one state must be recognized by courts in other states, ensuring that citizens cannot escape legal judgments simply by crossing state lines.

- **Public Acts and Records**: This clause also ensures that public documents, such as marriage licenses, birth certificates, and other state-issued records, are honored by other states. For example, a marriage legally performed in one state is recognized as valid in all other states, even if the laws governing marriage may vary from state to state.

This provision helps create a sense of national unity, as it removes barriers for citizens who move between states or engage in interstate commerce, knowing that their rights and obligations are upheld no matter where they are.

Privileges and Immunities

Section 2 of Article IV addresses the **privileges and immunities** that citizens enjoy when they move from one state to another. This clause ensures that a citizen of one state has the same fundamental rights and protections in other states as they would in their home state. It is a critical part of the Constitution's effort to promote equality and prevent discrimination based on state residency.

- **Equal Treatment**: Citizens are entitled to the same privileges and immunities that the residents of a state enjoy, such as the right to own property, work, or access public services. For example, a person from California who moves to Texas cannot be denied the right to work in Texas simply because they are not a Texas resident.

- **Exceptions**: However, this clause allows states to impose certain restrictions if they serve a legitimate state interest. For instance, a state may charge out-of-state residents higher tuition at public universities than in-state residents, as long as the policy has a reasonable justification.

This section protects citizens from discrimination as they travel and move across the country, fostering a sense of fairness and ensuring that they are not unfairly disadvantaged simply because they come from a different state.

New States and Territories

Section 3 of Article IV grants Congress the authority to admit new states into the Union and regulate the territories. This section lays the foundation for the expansion of the United States, providing a clear path for new territories to become states. The process requires federal approval, ensuring that the creation of new states aligns with the nation's interests and the established legal framework.

- **Admission of New States**: Congress has the power to admit new states, and no new state can be created within the jurisdiction of an existing state without that state's consent. This clause was particularly important during westward expansion, as it ensured that new territories could eventually join the Union while maintaining existing states' rights and boundaries.

- **Territorial Regulation**: While the Constitution grants Congress the authority to admit states, it also gives Congress the power to govern U.S. territories. This provision allowed the federal government to manage land acquisitions and territories before they became states, as was the case with the territories gained through the Louisiana Purchase and the Mexican-American War.

This section ensures that new states are brought into the Union in an orderly, standardized process, while allowing the federal government to maintain control over territories until they are ready for statehood.

Federal Protection of States

Section 4 of Article IV requires the federal government to guarantee that each state has a **republican form of government** and provides for federal protection in times of invasion or domestic unrest.

- **Republican Form of Government**: The federal government guarantees that each state will have a government that is representative and democratic. This was intended to prevent any state from establishing a monarchy or dictatorship. It ensures that every state's government is grounded in the principles of popular sovereignty, where authority is derived from the people.

- **Protection from Invasion and Domestic Violence**: The federal government is responsible for protecting states from invasion. If a state is invaded by a foreign power or faces an insurrection, it is the duty of the federal government to step in and provide defense and support. In addition, if a state requests help to suppress domestic violence (such as rebellion or civil unrest), the federal government has the authority to intervene and restore order.

This section ensures that states are not left vulnerable to threats, either from external forces or internal turmoil, and that the federal government plays a crucial role in ensuring the stability and security of the nation as a whole.

Article IV establishes the relationship between the states and the federal government, as well as the relationships between individual states. By addressing the recognition of legal decisions across state lines, ensuring that citizens have equal rights in all states, and providing for the orderly admission of new states, the article fosters unity and cooperation between states. The federal government's role in guaranteeing a republican form of government and offering protection from invasion or domestic violence further strengthens the bonds between the states and the nation as a whole.

This article reflects the framers' vision of a balanced, interconnected Union—one that respects the rights of individual states but also ensures that they operate as part of a cohesive, united whole.

Article V: Amending the Constitution

Article V of the U.S. Constitution sets out the procedures for amending the Constitution, allowing it to adapt over time while maintaining its stability and foundational principles. The amendment process is intentionally rigorous to ensure that any changes to the Constitution reflect broad consensus and long-term agreement. This deliberate difficulty safeguards the Constitution against hasty or temporary changes, ensuring its enduring relevance in a changing society.

The Amendment Process

The process for amending the Constitution is intentionally challenging to ensure that amendments are not made impulsively or for fleeting political reasons. The two primary methods for proposing and ratifying amendments are as follows:

1. **Proposal by Congress**: The first and most commonly used method for proposing an amendment is for Congress to introduce it. This requires a two-thirds majority vote in both the **House of Representatives** and the **Senate**. This high threshold ensures that only proposals with significant bipartisan support are put forward. Once passed by both chambers of Congress, the proposed amendment moves to the states for ratification.

2. **Proposal by a Constitutional Convention**: The second method for proposing an amendment allows for a **constitutional convention** to be called. This is

triggered if two-thirds of state legislatures (34 out of 50 states) request it. The convention would convene to propose amendments. While this method has never been used, it serves as a safeguard, allowing states to push for significant constitutional changes if they believe Congress is unwilling to do so.

Once an amendment has been proposed through one of these two methods, it must be ratified to become part of the Constitution.

Ratification of Amendments

Once an amendment is proposed, it must be ratified by the states. Ratification requires the approval of **three-fourths of the state legislatures** (38 out of 50 states) or by **ratifying conventions** in three-fourths of the states, as determined by Congress. This high bar ensures that proposed amendments are widely accepted by the nation as a whole, not just by a narrow group of states or political interests.

- **State Legislatures vs. Conventions**: Congress can choose whether the ratification will occur in state legislatures or through state conventions. While the legislative process is more commonly used, the option for conventions was included to provide flexibility in case state legislatures were unwilling to ratify significant constitutional changes.

Flexibility and Stability

The difficulty of the amendment process ensures that the Constitution is not easily altered. This reflects the framers' belief that the Constitution should be able to adapt to changing times and evolving values, but that changes should only happen with widespread support. This system provides both **flexibility** and **stability**: the Constitution can evolve in response to new challenges, but only when there is a broad, national consensus that such changes are necessary.

The framers also recognized that future generations might need to address problems that could not have been foreseen in 1787. The amendment process allows for such changes, but it is designed to protect the core principles of the document from being easily overridden by political pressures or short-term desires.

Article VI: Supremacy, Oaths, and Public Trust

Article VI of the U.S. Constitution contains provisions that emphasize the **supremacy** of federal law, the **oaths of office** taken by public officials, and the prohibition of religious tests for officeholders. These provisions were written to ensure that the Constitution remains the supreme law of the land, that public officials act in accordance with the principles of the Constitution, and that government remains inclusive and accountable to all citizens.

The Supremacy Clause

The **Supremacy Clause** in Section 2 of Article VI is one of the most important provisions in the Constitution. It states:

"This Constitution, and the Laws of the United States which shall be made in Pursuance thereof; and all Treaties made, or which shall be made, under the Authority of the United States, shall be the supreme Law of the Land; and the Judges in every State shall be bound thereby, any Thing in the Constitution or Laws of any State to the Contrary notwithstanding."

This clause establishes that the **Constitution**, as well as laws and treaties made under its authority, are the **supreme law of the land**. It requires that **state courts** and **state governments** adhere to federal law when there is a conflict.

- **Federal Over State Law**: The Supremacy Clause effectively means that if state laws or state constitutions contradict federal laws or the

Constitution, **federal law takes precedence**. This principle ensures that the United States operates under a unified legal framework, preventing states from creating laws that undermine national unity or conflict with federal policies.

- **Uniformity Across the Nation**: This clause prevents legal confusion and inconsistency by ensuring that the same laws apply equally to all citizens across every state. For example, if federal civil rights laws are enacted, state laws cannot override or circumvent those protections.

- **Judicial Authority**: Judges in all states are required to uphold the Constitution and federal laws, even if state laws conflict with them. This creates a consistent and unified legal system across the country, ensuring fairness and equality for all citizens.

The Supremacy Clause is a cornerstone of federalism, which balances the powers of state and national government. It ensures that the United States operates under a single set of fundamental laws, while still allowing for state autonomy in areas not addressed by federal law.

Oaths of Office

Section 3 of Article VI mandates that all public officials, including members of Congress, the president, and federal judges, must take an **oath of office** to support and defend the Constitution. This requirement reinforces the principle of accountability and underscores the importance of loyalty to the Constitution above all else.

- **Oath of Allegiance**: The oath ensures that all public officials pledge to uphold the Constitution and carry out their duties in accordance with its principles. This creates a uniform standard for public service and reinforces the idea that officials act in the public interest, not in their own personal or political interests.

- **Presidential and Judicial Oaths**: The president, members of Congress, and federal judges take similar oaths, ensuring that they are all held to the same standard of loyalty to the Constitution. These oaths provide a foundation of trust, ensuring that those in power are committed to protecting and preserving the rights and freedoms enshrined in the Constitution.

Religious Test Prohibition

The final clause in Article VI explicitly prohibits **religious tests** for any officeholder in the United States government:

"but no religious Test shall ever be required as a Qualification to any Office or public Trust under the United States."

This provision reflects the framers' commitment to **religious freedom** and ensures that no individual is barred from holding public office because of their religious beliefs (or lack thereof). It is a crucial safeguard for the separation of church and state and protects the rights of citizens to serve their country, regardless of their faith.

- **Inclusivity in Government**: This clause ensures that people of all religious beliefs—or no religious belief at all—can serve in government. It was a rejection of the practice in many European countries where religious tests were used to determine who could hold office, a practice the framers saw as unjust and discriminatory.

- **Equality Before the Law**: By preventing religious tests, this provision affirms that all citizens are equal under the law, and that the government should not favor one religion over another. It ensures that religious freedom is respected in both public and private life, and that government positions are open to all qualified citizens.

Article VI of the Constitution serves to reinforce the **supremacy of federal law**, the **accountability** of public officials to the Constitution, and the **protection of religious freedom** in government. The Supremacy Clause ensures that the nation operates under a consistent legal framework, while the oath of office provides a basis for public trust in government officials. The prohibition of religious tests ensures that government remains inclusive, upholding the principles of equality and religious liberty that are central to American identity. Together, these provisions maintain the integrity and stability of the U.S. government and protect the rights of its citizens.

Article VII: Ratification

Article VII of the U.S. Constitution lays out the formal process for its ratification, providing the legal framework for how the Constitution would transition from a proposal to the governing document of the United States. This article is foundational because it outlines how the Constitution would come into effect and establishes the criteria for approval. It was the final section of the original document, and it marked the culmination of the work done at the Constitutional Convention in 1787.

The Ratification Process

Article VII outlines the specific procedures by which the new Constitution would be ratified. This process was designed to allow the Constitution to gain the necessary support from the states, particularly through a process that was intended to be both efficient and democratic.

- **Ratification by Conventions**: The Constitution would not be ratified by state legislatures, as was the case with most legal documents at the time, but by special **ratifying conventions**. Each state would hold a convention, specifically convened to decide whether or not to adopt the new Constitution. This was a crucial decision, as it allowed the people of the states, through their elected representatives, to directly decide the fate of the Constitution. The framers were concerned that the existing state legislatures, which had operated under the Articles of Confederation, might not want to relinquish the limited powers they had held and might resist adopting a new, stronger central government.

- o **Why Conventions?**: The decision to have conventions, rather than legislative bodies, ratify the Constitution was a bold choice. The framers believed that it would be too difficult to get the approval of state legislatures, as many were invested in the existing system and were wary of a more centralized government. By convening special ratifying conventions, the framers aimed to bypass the traditional political institutions that might oppose the changes.

- o **Democratic Legitimacy**: The choice of conventions was also a decision to involve the people more directly. State legislatures were often controlled by elites, and the framers wanted the Constitution to have greater democratic legitimacy. By putting the decision in the hands of the people through their representatives in the conventions, the Constitution would have a broader mandate and would be more likely to gain widespread acceptance across the states.

Ratification Threshold: Nine States

One of the most critical aspects of Article VII is its provision regarding the number of states required for ratification. The Constitution would come into effect once **nine out of thirteen states** had ratified it. This was a carefully calculated decision, as it balanced the need for broad support with the reality of the strong opposition that the Constitution was likely to face in some states.

- **Nine States Requirement**: The framers knew that unanimity among the 13 states would be difficult to achieve. By setting the bar at nine states, they created a practical threshold that would allow the new government to begin functioning while still ensuring that the Constitution had broad national support. If the document had required unanimous approval, it might never have been adopted. Nine states was seen as a sufficiently strong majority to move forward, without requiring all the states to agree.

  - ○ **Political Strategy**: This provision reflected a pragmatic understanding of the political landscape. While all states were expected to eventually join the Union under the new Constitution, setting the threshold at nine allowed for early adoption without waiting for full consensus. It was an acknowledgment that some states, particularly those that had strong loyalty to the Articles of Confederation, might resist the changes.

  - ○ **Early Adopters**: The first states to ratify the Constitution were Delaware, Pennsylvania, New Jersey, Georgia, and Connecticut, who all ratified relatively quickly. These states were generally more eager for the kind of strong central government the Constitution proposed. However, some states, including **Massachusetts, Virginia**, and **New York**, initially hesitated, and only agreed to ratify after being promised that a Bill of Rights would be added to protect individual liberties.

The Role of the Signatories

Article VII also includes a list of signatories—the individuals who signed the Constitution after its drafting at the Constitutional Convention. The article states that the Constitution was **signed by the delegates present at the convention** in Philadelphia, with **George Washington** presiding over the proceedings.

- **Who Signed?**: The signatories of the Constitution included key figures such as **Benjamin Franklin, James Madison, Alexander Hamilton**, and others. These men were central to the drafting process and played pivotal roles in shaping the final document. However, some notable figures, such as **Thomas Jefferson** and **John Adams**, were absent from the Constitutional Convention, as they were serving abroad as diplomats.

  o **Unity and Division**: The act of signing the document was not without division. Some delegates, such as **Edmund Randolph** and **George Mason** of Virginia, refused to sign because they felt the Constitution gave too much power to the national government and lacked sufficient protections for individual rights. This division in the signing of the document reflects the deep concerns that some had about the proposed system. Despite this, the majority of delegates chose to sign in the belief that the Constitution was the best option for the country.

- **Historical Significance**: The act of signing was symbolic, representing the beginning of a new chapter for the United States. The signatories were agreeing to put the framework of government in the hands of the states, trusting that the document they had crafted would gain the necessary support and be implemented as the new law of the land.

Ratification by the States: The Road to Adoption

Though the initial process was set in motion with Article VII, the road to full ratification was not smooth. Some states were initially hesitant to ratify the Constitution and raised concerns about its balance of power and lack of protections for individual liberties. The debates and eventual ratification process unfolded as follows:

- **Massachusetts and Virginia**: These were two of the largest and most influential states, and their support was crucial to the Constitution's success. Massachusetts ratified the Constitution after a promise that a Bill of Rights would be added. Similarly, Virginia's ratification was contingent on a strong commitment to including protections for individual liberties.

- **New York and Rhode Island**: These two states held out the longest. New York ratified the Constitution only after intense debate and the persuasive arguments of **Alexander Hamilton** and **John Jay**, who wrote the **Federalist Papers** to support ratification. Rhode Island, the last state to ratify, held out until 1790, long after the new government had already begun functioning.

The Significance of Article VII

Article VII is a key element in the transition from the Articles of Confederation to the new federal system established by the Constitution. It provided the legal process for turning the proposal into law. The decision to allow for ratification by conventions was a groundbreaking step in American democracy, ensuring that the people would have the final say.

- **Shaping the Nation's Future**: The success of the ratification process was not inevitable. The process required significant compromise, negotiation, and political maneuvering. The decision to make the Constitution the supreme law of the land, once ratified by a sufficient number of states, was an early example of how the nation would work to form a more perfect union.

- **Long-Term Impact**: The Constitution was ratified and implemented beginning in 1788, and it remains the governing document of the United States today. Article VII ensured that the adoption of the Constitution would be legitimate, democratic, and reflect a nationwide consensus, even though some states initially resisted it.

Article VII stands as the concluding chapter of the Constitution's creation, establishing the necessary framework for its adoption. By specifying that the Constitution would take effect once nine states had ratified it, and by allowing for conventions to directly decide its fate, Article VII reflects the importance of popular sovereignty and democratic legitimacy in the nation's foundational document. The ratification process was a critical step in uniting the states under a single, stronger government, and it marked the beginning of a new chapter in American governance.

Part IV: The Bill of Rights Explained

Why the Bill of Rights Was Added

The Bill of Rights, consisting of the first ten amendments to the U.S. Constitution, serves as a cornerstone of American democracy, providing essential protections for individual liberties and limiting the power of government. The addition of the Bill of Rights was not an inevitable part of the original Constitutional plan but rather a direct response to widespread concerns about the potential for government overreach and the protection of personal freedoms.

Context and Historical Background

When the U.S. Constitution was initially drafted in 1787 and ratified in 1788, it established a strong federal government. However, it lacked specific protections for individual rights and liberties. The Constitution's framers were deeply concerned with creating a balanced government—one strong enough to govern effectively but not so powerful that it would infringe upon the freedoms of the people. They believed that the structure of the Constitution, with its separation of powers, checks and balances, and enumeration of government powers, would inherently limit government overreach.

Yet, many Americans feared that the new government would still be able to infringe upon their natural rights.

These fears were especially strong in states like **Massachusetts**, **Virginia**, and **New York**, where influential figures and political leaders argued that the Constitution should explicitly guarantee individual freedoms. They were worried that without these explicit protections, the new government could become tyrannical, just as they had feared under British rule.

The debate over the inclusion of a Bill of Rights became a major point of contention during the ratification process of the Constitution. Many states agreed to ratify the document with the understanding that a Bill of Rights would be added shortly afterward.

The Federalists vs. The Anti-Federalists

The **Federalists**, those who supported the new Constitution, believed that the structure of the document itself offered sufficient protections against tyranny. They argued that the Constitution's design—including the division of powers, the system of checks and balances, and the ability of the people to elect their representatives—was enough to safeguard individual liberties. They feared that enumerating specific rights could be dangerous because it might imply that rights not mentioned were not protected.

On the other hand, the **Anti-Federalists**, who opposed the Constitution, believed that without a clear, written guarantee of individual rights, the government could easily trample on the freedoms of the people. They worried that the Constitution did not go far enough in protecting fundamental rights such as freedom of speech, the press, and religion, the right to a fair trial, and the right to bear arms.

To resolve this conflict and ensure the Constitution's ratification, Federalist leaders, including **James Madison**, promised to add a Bill of Rights. This assurance was crucial in securing the support of key states, such as **Virginia**, **Massachusetts**, and **New York**, which were essential for the Constitution's adoption.

The Role of James Madison and the First Congress

James Madison, often called the "Father of the Constitution," played a pivotal role in drafting the Bill of Rights. Although he had initially argued against the need for a Bill of Rights, believing the Constitution's structure was sufficient, he ultimately became its strongest advocate in Congress. Madison believed that a Bill of Rights would help ensure the rights of individuals were explicitly protected, and it would address the concerns of Anti-Federalists, making the Constitution more widely acceptable.

Madison introduced a series of proposed amendments in **1789** to the first **Congress**. These proposals were based on recommendations from state ratifying conventions and influenced by earlier documents like the **Virginia Declaration of Rights** and the **English Bill of Rights**. After extensive debate and revision, the **House of Representatives** approved twelve amendments, which were sent to the states for ratification.

The final **ten amendments** were ratified by the required three-fourths of state legislatures in **1791**, and they became the **Bill of Rights**. These amendments sought to protect individual liberties, limit government power, and address the concerns raised by Anti-Federalists.

The Major Concerns Addressed by the Bill of Rights

The Bill of Rights addresses many of the fears that led to its creation, including the need for protections against governmental abuses of power. Some of the key concerns addressed by the Bill of Rights include:

1. **Protection of Individual Liberties**: The first ten amendments explicitly protect fundamental freedoms, such as freedom of speech, freedom of the press, freedom of religion, the right to assembly, and the right to petition the government. These provisions ensure that individuals can express themselves, practice their religion freely, and hold the government accountable without fear of persecution or punishment.

2. **Limitation on Government Power**: Many of the amendments were designed to limit the reach of government. For example, the **Third Amendment** prevents the government from forcing citizens to quarter soldiers in their homes, a grievance that had been common during British rule. The **Fourth Amendment** protects citizens against unreasonable searches and seizures, ensuring that the government cannot invade personal privacy without just cause.

3. **Due Process and Fair Treatment**: Amendments such as the **Fifth**, **Sixth**, **Seventh**, and **Eighth** provide protections related to criminal justice. They ensure that individuals are treated fairly by the legal system, including protections against double jeopardy, self-incrimination, and cruel and unusual

punishment. The right to a speedy and public trial by an impartial jury is guaranteed, ensuring that accused individuals receive a fair trial.

4. **State Power vs. Federal Power:** The **Tenth Amendment** emphasizes the principle of federalism by stating that powers not granted to the federal government or prohibited to the states by the Constitution are reserved for the states or the people. This helps maintain the balance of power between state and federal governments, preventing overreach by the national government.

The Bill of Rights and the Expansion of Rights

While the Bill of Rights was originally intended to limit the federal government's powers, it has had a much broader impact over time. Through the doctrine of **incorporation**, the protections provided by the Bill of Rights have been applied to state governments through the **Fourteenth Amendment's** Equal Protection and Due Process Clauses. This means that many of the rights guaranteed in the Bill of Rights, such as the freedom of speech or the right to a fair trial, apply not just at the federal level but also in state courts and state governments.

Over the years, the Bill of Rights has been expanded through judicial interpretation, legislative action, and constitutional amendments to ensure a more inclusive understanding of individual rights. For example, the **Nineteenth Amendment** granted women the right to vote, and the **Civil Rights Movement** led to landmark legal changes, such as the **Civil Rights Act of 1964**, which further expanded civil rights protections.

The Bill of Rights Today

The Bill of Rights remains as relevant today as it was in 1791. It continues to serve as the bedrock of American law and serves as the standard by which the nation measures its respect for personal freedoms and democratic principles. Its protections are constantly cited in legal cases, public debates, and political discussions, ensuring that the rights of citizens remain a central concern of American governance.

The Bill of Rights has become a symbol of the nation's commitment to freedom, justice, and equality. It reminds us that the government exists to serve the people, not the other way around. It is a powerful testament to the enduring belief in the fundamental rights of individuals, safeguarding them from government overreach and securing the freedoms that are central to the American experience.

The Bill of Rights was added to the Constitution to address the fears and concerns of those who believed that the new government might become tyrannical or oppressive, as they had experienced under British rule. By providing explicit protections for individual liberties and limiting the power of government, the Bill of Rights became an essential part of the American political system.

Its addition was a necessary compromise to secure the Constitution's ratification and to ensure that the new government would be accountable to the people it governed. The Bill of Rights continues to serve as a crucial safeguard against the potential abuse of power, reminding us of the fundamental freedoms that are at the heart of American democracy.

Amendment I: Religion, Speech, Press, Assembly, Petition

The **First Amendment** is one of the most crucial elements of the Bill of Rights, as it safeguards the fundamental freedoms essential to democracy. It protects five specific freedoms—**religion, speech, press, assembly,** and **petition**—which form the foundation of American civil liberties and democratic governance. These freedoms allow individuals to express their opinions, practice their religion freely, access information, gather in protest, and demand changes in government, ensuring a vibrant and participatory society.

Freedom of Religion

The First Amendment guarantees the **freedom of religion,** ensuring that individuals are free to practice their religion without government interference. This provision serves two key functions:

1. **Establishment Clause**: The government is prohibited from establishing an official religion or showing preferential treatment toward one religion over others. This prevents the government from endorsing or funding religious practices, ensuring a separation of church and state. It is often interpreted as a safeguard against theocracy, ensuring that no religion can dominate the public sphere.

2. **Free Exercise Clause**: This part of the amendment protects individuals' rights to practice their religion

freely. It ensures that individuals can worship, express religious beliefs, and practice their faith without fear of government reprisal. The government cannot prevent the free exercise of religion unless doing so would harm others or violate other established laws.

This dual protection of religious freedom was crucial in the founding of the United States, especially given the nation's diverse religious makeup and the early history of religious persecution.

Freedom of Speech

The **freedom of speech** is one of the most vital and contested rights in American society. It protects the right of individuals to express themselves without fear of government censorship or punishment. This includes the right to speak freely in public, as well as the right to express opinions on a variety of topics—political, social, and cultural.

- **Political Speech**: The First Amendment places particular importance on **political speech**, as it enables individuals to criticize the government, express dissent, and advocate for change. This protection ensures that citizens can challenge government actions, propose alternatives, and engage in public debates without fear of repression. The right to criticize the government is a cornerstone of a healthy democracy.

- **Limitations on Speech**: While the First Amendment guarantees free speech, this right is not absolute. There are limitations, such as speech that incites imminent lawless action (**Brandenburg v. Ohio**, 1969), speech that defames others (**libel and slander**), and speech that poses a direct threat to national security (**like shouting "fire" in a crowded theater when there is no fire**). Courts have established a framework for balancing free expression with the protection of public safety and other individuals' rights.

Freedom of the Press

The **freedom of the press** ensures that the press can report news and express opinions without government censorship or control. It allows the media to act as a watchdog, scrutinizing government actions, exposing corruption, and informing the public. This freedom is crucial for the functioning of a democratic society because it helps keep the government accountable and provides citizens with the information necessary to make informed decisions.

- **Protection of Journalists**: The press freedom ensures that journalists, news organizations, and media outlets can operate freely without government interference or retaliation. It allows for the publication of news, investigative reports, and commentary without fear of censorship, fines, or imprisonment.

- **Prior Restraint**: The courts have consistently interpreted the First Amendment as prohibiting **prior restraint**, which is the government's action to prevent publication before it occurs. For instance, the **Pentagon Papers case** (**New York Times Co. v. United States**, 1971) reinforced the principle that the government cannot stop the press from publishing materials, even if it is critical of government policies, unless it can prove a significant risk to national security.

Freedom of Assembly

The **freedom of assembly** guarantees the right of individuals to gather peacefully in groups for any purpose—whether political, social, or religious. It protects the right of citizens to organize protests, rallies, or demonstrations, which has historically been essential for social and political movements.

- **Peaceful Protest**: This right allows people to express collective opinions and grievances. The **Civil Rights Movement** and other social justice movements, for example, relied heavily on this right to organize protests and demand legislative change.

- **Government Regulation**: While the government cannot prohibit assembly, it can impose certain **time, place, and manner restrictions** to ensure that public safety is maintained and that assemblies do not interfere with other essential activities. These regulations must be **content-neutral**, meaning they cannot be used to stifle particular messages or viewpoints.

Freedom to Petition the Government

The **freedom to petition** guarantees that individuals can approach the government with complaints, grievances, or requests for change, without fear of punishment or retaliation. This right allows citizens to seek redress for perceived wrongs and to advocate for policy changes.

- **Right to Lobby and Petition**: Whether through petitions, protests, or formal lobbying, citizens have the right to ask their government to act on issues they care about. This right is vital for maintaining a government that is responsive to its people's needs and concerns.

The First Amendment is a cornerstone of American democracy, safeguarding the rights to freedom of religion, speech, the press, peaceful assembly, and petitioning the government. These freedoms are essential for allowing citizens to express their views, challenge authority, and participate in the democratic process. Although these rights are not without limits, they form the bedrock of individual liberty in the United States and are key to the functioning of a free and open society.

Amendment II: The Right to Keep and Bear Arms

The **Second Amendment** protects the right of individuals to keep and bear arms. This amendment is often one of the most contentious in American law, as it intersects with issues of public safety, individual rights, and the role of government. It is succinctly stated as follows:

"A well-regulated Militia, being necessary to the security of a free State, the right of the people to keep and bear Arms, shall not be infringed."

The Militia and the Right to Bear Arms

The Second Amendment contains two key components:

1. **The Militia Clause**: The phrase "A well-regulated Militia, being necessary to the security of a free State" reflects the framers' concern with a citizen militia for national defense. In the late 18th century, the idea of a **well-regulated militia** was vital to the nation's defense. The United States did not have a standing army, and state militias were viewed as essential for protecting the nation and maintaining order.

2. **The Right to Bear Arms**: The second clause—"the right of the people to keep and bear Arms, shall not be infringed"—secures an individual right to possess and carry firearms. This provision has been interpreted in various ways, but it is generally seen

as guaranteeing an individual's right to own firearms, independent of service in a militia.

Interpretations and Legal Precedent

The exact scope of the Second Amendment has been the subject of extensive debate and legal interpretation. For many years, the **Supreme Court** treated the right to bear arms as primarily related to **military service**. However, this changed with the landmark **District of Columbia v. Heller** decision in 2008, which interpreted the Second Amendment as protecting an individual's right to possess firearms for self-defense, particularly within their homes. This ruling marked a significant shift toward recognizing the individual right to bear arms, separate from the concept of a militia.

The Debate on Gun Rights

The Second Amendment has sparked intense debate, especially regarding gun control. Advocates for broader gun rights argue that the right to bear arms is fundamental to personal liberty, self-defense, and the protection of democracy against tyranny. They believe that law-abiding citizens should have the ability to own firearms, including handguns and rifles.

Conversely, proponents of gun control argue that more regulation is necessary to protect public safety. They emphasize the rising incidence of gun violence, mass shootings, and the need to strike a balance between individual rights and the welfare of society as a whole. Laws regulating firearm ownership, such as background checks, restrictions on assault weapons, and waiting periods, are often proposed as means to reduce gun violence while still respecting the right to bear arms.

The Second Amendment guarantees the individual right to keep and bear arms, a right that remains central to American culture and politics. While the precise boundaries of this right continue to evolve through judicial interpretation and legislation, the amendment reflects the framers' intent to preserve personal freedoms and ensure the ability of citizens to defend themselves and their nation. The debate surrounding the Second Amendment illustrates the ongoing tension between individual rights and public safety in American society, making it one of the most contested and important parts of the Bill of Rights.

Amendment III: Quartering of Soldiers

The **Third Amendment** of the U.S. Constitution addresses a concern that arose during the colonial period and was rooted in the experiences of American colonists under British rule. It prohibits the government from forcing citizens to house (or "quarter") soldiers in their homes during times of peace or war, except in a manner prescribed by law. The exact text of the amendment reads:

"No Soldier shall, in time of peace be quartered in any house, without the consent of the Owner, nor in time of war, but in a manner to be prescribed by law."

Historical Context: British Practices

The Third Amendment was a direct response to the practice of **quartering soldiers** that was common under British rule before and during the American Revolution. Under the **Quartering Acts** passed by the British Parliament, American colonists were required to provide food, shelter, and other provisions for British soldiers stationed in the colonies. This practice was seen as a violation of the colonists' privacy and property rights, and it contributed to the growing resentment toward British authority. The colonists viewed this as an abuse of power, one that infringed on their rights as Englishmen.

The Core Protection

The Third Amendment protects individuals' right to privacy in their homes and ensures that citizens cannot be forced to host military personnel without their consent. It does so in two key ways:

1. **In Time of Peace**: The amendment specifically forbids the quartering of soldiers in private homes during times of peace. This provision is meant to protect the sanctity of one's home and property from government intrusion during non-emergency periods.

2. **In Time of War**: The amendment allows for the possibility of quartering soldiers during times of war, but only under strict conditions and according to procedures laid out by law. This ensures that, in extreme circumstances, such as during wartime, the government may have the authority to house soldiers in private residences, but only if it is clearly authorized by legislation. This was intended to limit the potential for abuse by requiring a legal framework to justify such an action.

The Amendment's Relevance Today

Although the Third Amendment is not frequently the subject of legal disputes, its inclusion in the Bill of Rights signifies the framers' commitment to protecting personal property and privacy against government overreach. It also reflects the broader principles of **individual liberty** and **protection from government intrusion**, which remain central to American legal and political thought.

In modern times, the Third Amendment has not been the subject of much litigation, as the issue of quartering soldiers has not been a significant concern since the time of the

American Revolution. However, it continues to serve as a symbolic and historical reminder of the need to limit the power of the government, particularly in relation to personal privacy and property rights.

The Third Amendment enshrines the principle that the government cannot impose itself into citizens' homes without their consent, except in specific, lawful circumstances. Though it was a response to the practices of the British, its inclusion in the Bill of Rights was crucial for laying the foundation for personal privacy and limiting government intrusion in the lives of American citizens. It remains a reminder of the importance of protecting the sanctity of the home and preventing the government from overreaching in times of peace and war.

Amendment IV: Searches, Seizures, and Warrants

The **Fourth Amendment** of the U.S. Constitution provides one of the most important protections for individual privacy and liberty. It protects citizens from unreasonable searches and seizures by the government and sets strict requirements for the issuance of warrants. The text of the Fourth Amendment reads:

"The right of the people to be secure in their persons, houses, papers, and effects, against unreasonable searches and seizures, shall not be violated, and no Warrants shall issue, but upon probable cause, supported by Oath or affirmation, and particularly describing the place to be searched, and the persons or things to be seized."

The Right to Privacy and Protection from Government Intrusion

The Fourth Amendment reflects the framers' understanding of the need to protect the privacy of individuals and their property from government overreach. The primary concern was to prevent the government from acting arbitrarily or indiscriminately when conducting searches or seizures. The amendment reflects a deep mistrust of unchecked government power, particularly following the abuses experienced under British rule, where soldiers and officials would often conduct searches without legal justification.

The protections provided by the Fourth Amendment ensure that individuals can live free from constant government surveillance or the threat of unwarranted intrusions into their private lives. The key aspects of the Fourth Amendment include:

1. **Protection Against Unreasonable Searches and Seizures**: The Fourth Amendment provides that individuals are **secure in their persons, houses, papers, and effects**. This broad language ensures that a wide range of personal property and aspects of an individual's life are protected from arbitrary government interference.

2. **Warrant Requirement**: In order to search a person or their property, the government must obtain a **warrant**. Warrants can only be issued by a judge or magistrate and must be based on **probable cause**, meaning there must be a reasonable belief that a crime has been committed or that evidence of a crime will be found in the location to be searched.

Probable Cause and Judicial Oversight

The requirement of **probable cause** and **judicial oversight** is central to the Fourth Amendment's protections. **Probable cause** means that law enforcement must have sufficient evidence to believe that a crime has been committed or that evidence of a crime is located at the place to be searched. This standard prevents the government from conducting random or speculative searches.

- **Judicial Approval**: Warrants must be obtained through a formal process and are subject to judicial review. This ensures that a neutral party (the judge) is involved in determining whether a search or seizure is justified, providing a safeguard against government abuse.

- **Particularity Requirement**: The Fourth Amendment also specifies that the warrant must be **specific** in nature, clearly identifying the location to be searched and the items or individuals to be seized. This requirement ensures that searches are not overly broad and that individuals are not subjected to searches for items or evidence unrelated to the original cause.

Exceptions to the Warrant Requirement

While the Fourth Amendment establishes strong protections against unreasonable searches and seizures, there are certain exceptions where a warrant is not required. These include:

1. **Consent Searches**: If an individual voluntarily consents to a search, no warrant is necessary. However, consent must be given freely and without coercion.

2. **Exigent Circumstances**: In emergency situations, where evidence may be destroyed or a suspect may flee, law enforcement may conduct searches without a warrant. These circumstances are narrowly defined and typically require immediate action.

3. **Searches Incident to Arrest**: When a person is arrested, law enforcement is allowed to search their person and the area within their immediate control to ensure safety and preserve evidence.

4. **Plain View Doctrine**: If law enforcement officers are lawfully present in a location and see evidence of a crime in plain view, they can seize the evidence without a warrant.

5. **Automobile Searches**: Due to the mobility of vehicles, law enforcement can search a vehicle without a warrant if they have probable cause to believe it contains evidence of a crime.

The Evolution of the Fourth Amendment

Over time, the **Supreme Court** has interpreted the Fourth Amendment to adapt to changing technologies and societal concerns. For instance, the **use of wiretaps**, **electronic surveillance**, and **GPS tracking** has raised new questions about the scope of privacy in the digital age. The Court has had to reconcile these technologies with the protections guaranteed by the Fourth Amendment, ensuring that privacy rights are not eroded by advances in technology.

The **exclusionary rule**, established through decisions like **Mapp v. Ohio** (1961), has also played a significant role in enforcing the Fourth Amendment. This rule holds that evidence obtained through unlawful searches or seizures is generally inadmissible in court. This serves as a deterrent against illegal police conduct and reinforces the importance of constitutional protections.

The Fourth Amendment stands as a vital protection for personal privacy and individual rights. By requiring that searches and seizures be reasonable and supported by probable cause, it ensures that citizens are protected from arbitrary government actions. The requirement for judicial oversight through warrants further ensures that there are checks and balances in the process of law enforcement. Over time, the Fourth Amendment has been critical in balancing law enforcement needs with the fundamental rights of individuals, and it remains an essential safeguard of liberty in the United States.

Amendment V: Due Process and Property Rights

The **Fifth Amendment** of the U.S. Constitution is a cornerstone of the American legal system. It protects several fundamental rights, including the right to **due process of law**, the protection against **self-incrimination**, the prohibition of **double jeopardy**, and safeguards regarding **property rights**. These protections ensure that individuals are treated fairly by the legal system and that government power is not abused.

The Right to Due Process

The due process clause is one of the most important provisions in the Fifth Amendment. It guarantees that no person shall be "deprived of life, liberty, or property, without due process of law." This means that the government cannot take away a person's rights or property without following a fair and established legal procedure.

- **Procedural Due Process**: This refers to the requirement that the government must follow fair procedures when it seeks to deprive an individual of their rights or property. These procedures must be transparent and consistent. For example, a person facing criminal charges must be given notice of the charges, an opportunity to be heard, and a fair trial. The concept of procedural due process ensures that individuals are treated fairly by the government and that laws are applied equally.

- **Substantive Due Process**: This aspect of due process protects certain fundamental rights from government interference, even if the procedures are fair. It ensures that certain rights—such as the right to marry, the right to raise children, and the right to privacy—cannot be infringed upon by the government, except in exceptional circumstances. The Supreme Court has interpreted the due process clause to cover these "fundamental rights" that are deeply rooted in the nation's history and traditions.

Protection Against Self-Incrimination

The Fifth Amendment also guarantees protection against **self-incrimination**. It states that no person "shall be compelled in any criminal case to be a witness against himself." This protection is often referred to as the **right to remain silent**.

- **Miranda Rights**: This protection became widely known due to the **Miranda v. Arizona** (1966) decision, in which the U.S. Supreme Court ruled that criminal suspects must be informed of their rights to remain silent and to have an attorney during interrogation. The "Miranda warnings" ensure that suspects are aware of their constitutional rights before they are questioned by law enforcement.

- **Prevention of Forced Confessions**: The Fifth Amendment protects individuals from being coerced into confessing crimes they did not commit. It prevents law enforcement from using physical or psychological pressure to obtain confessions, ensuring that any statement made by a suspect is voluntary and not forced.

Protection Against Double Jeopardy

Another important provision in the Fifth Amendment is the protection against **double jeopardy**, which prohibits an individual from being tried twice for the same offense. This clause ensures that once a person has been acquitted or convicted, they cannot be put in jeopardy of punishment again for the same crime.

- **Finality of Verdicts**: Double jeopardy ensures that once a verdict has been reached—whether guilty or not guilty—there is closure. The government cannot repeatedly prosecute a person for the same offense in an attempt to secure a different outcome.

- **Exceptions**: Double jeopardy protections do not apply in every situation. For example, if a case is dismissed due to a mistrial or procedural error, a defendant can be retried. Additionally, a defendant can be prosecuted in both state and federal courts for the same offense, as they are separate legal systems, but this is not considered double jeopardy.

Protection of Property Rights

The Fifth Amendment also provides a key protection related to property rights. The government is prohibited from taking private property for public use without offering **just compensation**. This is known as the **eminent domain** clause.

- **Eminent Domain**: Under the principle of eminent domain, the government can take private property for public purposes, such as building roads, schools, or other public infrastructure. However, the government must provide fair compensation to the property owner, ensuring that individuals are not unfairly deprived of their property without just compensation.

- **Limitations on Government Power**: This provision limits the government's ability to take property for its own benefit. It ensures that the government cannot arbitrarily seize property from citizens without providing a fair and just reason for doing so, as well as adequate compensation.

The Fifth Amendment is a vital protection for individuals, ensuring fairness and justice in the legal system. It guards against government overreach, providing protections against self-incrimination, double jeopardy, and unjust deprivation of life, liberty, or property. By establishing due process, the amendment ensures that individuals are treated equitably under the law and that their rights are protected in both criminal and civil matters. It also establishes limits on the government's power, ensuring that property rights are respected and that citizens are not deprived of their possessions without proper compensation.

Amendment VI: Rights of the Accused

The **Sixth Amendment** is a key protection for individuals who are accused of crimes, ensuring that they are treated fairly in the criminal justice system. It lays out a series of fundamental rights that allow individuals to defend themselves against criminal charges, ensuring that trials are transparent, public, and fair.

Right to a Speedy and Public Trial

The Sixth Amendment guarantees that individuals accused of crimes have the right to a **speedy trial**. This protection prevents individuals from being held in jail for an extended period without a trial, ensuring that they are not subjected to undue punishment or anxiety while awaiting trial.

- **Speedy Trial**: The right to a speedy trial is meant to prevent prolonged detention and to ensure that criminal cases are handled in a timely manner. This helps avoid the potential for abuse of power and ensures that witnesses and evidence remain fresh.

- **Public Trial**: The Sixth Amendment also guarantees the right to a **public trial**, meaning that the proceedings of the trial are open to the public. This ensures transparency and accountability in the judicial system, allowing citizens to observe the legal process and ensuring that the accused receives a fair trial.

Right to an Impartial Jury

The Sixth Amendment guarantees the right to a trial by an **impartial jury**. This ensures that the jury members are unbiased and do not have any preconceived notions about the case. This protection is critical to ensuring fairness in the criminal justice process.

- **Jury of Peers**: The right to a jury of peers means that the jury will consist of individuals who are representative of the community in which the alleged crime occurred. This provides an important safeguard against bias and helps ensure that the accused is judged by a group of citizens who are not prejudiced.

Right to Be Informed of the Charges

The Sixth Amendment guarantees that individuals accused of a crime have the right to be informed of the **nature and cause** of the charges against them. This is a fundamental protection that ensures that individuals understand what they are being accused of and have the opportunity to prepare a defense.

- **Notice of Charges**: The government must provide a clear and detailed description of the charges so that the accused can respond appropriately. This ensures that the defendant is not left in the dark about the case they are facing and can make informed decisions about how to proceed.

Right to Confront Witnesses

The Sixth Amendment also guarantees the right to **confront witnesses** against the accused. This ensures that the defendant has the opportunity to cross-examine witnesses and challenge the evidence presented against them.

- **Cross-Examination**: The right to confront and cross-examine witnesses is a fundamental part of the adversarial legal system. It ensures that the accused has the opportunity to test the credibility and reliability of the testimony presented by the prosecution.

Right to Have Counsel

Perhaps one of the most important protections of the Sixth Amendment is the right to have **counsel** (a lawyer) for defense. If the accused cannot afford a lawyer, the government is required to provide one, ensuring that individuals are not deprived of their constitutional right to a fair defense due to financial limitations.

- **Right to Legal Representation**: The right to counsel ensures that individuals have access to legal expertise and guidance in defending themselves against criminal charges. Without this right, the justice system could unfairly disadvantage those who do not have the knowledge or resources to defend themselves effectively.

The Sixth Amendment is designed to ensure fairness and transparency in the criminal justice system. It protects the rights of the accused by guaranteeing a speedy trial, an impartial jury, the right to be informed of the charges, the right to confront witnesses, and the right to counsel. These protections are essential for ensuring that criminal trials are just and that individuals have a fair opportunity to defend themselves against accusations. Together with other amendments in the Bill of Rights, the Sixth Amendment helps safeguard the core principles of justice, equality, and individual rights.

Amendment VII: Civil Jury Trials

The **Seventh Amendment** of the U.S. Constitution guarantees the right to a **jury trial** in civil cases. This amendment ensures that individuals have the right to have their legal disputes settled by a jury of their peers, rather than solely by a judge. Civil cases typically involve disputes between private parties—whether individuals, organizations, or companies—regarding issues like contracts, property, and torts (wrongful acts).

The Text of the Seventh Amendment

The full text of the Seventh Amendment reads:

"In Suits at common law, where the value in controversy shall exceed twenty dollars, the right of trial by jury shall be preserved, and no fact tried by a jury shall be otherwise reexamined in any Court of the United States, than according to the rules of the common law."

This provision enshrines the right to a jury trial in **civil cases** and ensures that the right to trial by jury cannot be dismissed by the courts. While criminal cases are typically more prominent in public discussions, civil cases are also an essential part of the legal system, and the Seventh Amendment protects the **right of citizens** to have disputes resolved through a trial process that includes their peers.

The Right to a Jury Trial in Civil Cases

The Seventh Amendment specifically applies to **civil cases** based on the **common law**, which is law developed through judicial decisions rather than statutes. The right to a jury trial in civil cases was seen as a safeguard against the overreach of government power, ensuring that decisions made in the courtroom are grounded in the judgment of ordinary people rather than solely in the hands of judges or governmental authorities.

- **Common Law and Jury Trials**: The amendment preserves the right to a jury trial for **suits at common law**. Common law refers to legal traditions and principles that evolved from English law and were adopted in the U.S. during the early years of the republic. The Seventh Amendment reflects the historical importance of jury trials in English legal tradition, which were seen as essential to ensuring that ordinary citizens were involved in the judicial process.

- **$20 Threshold**: The clause specifying that the value in controversy must exceed **twenty dollars** was a relatively modest sum at the time the Constitution was written, designed to ensure that even small disputes could be heard by a jury. Although the exact value of twenty dollars would be worth far less today due to inflation, this provision was historically significant and remains part of the amendment as a symbol of the framers' intention to uphold the right to trial by jury in significant civil cases.

Limitations and Modern Application

While the Seventh Amendment guarantees the right to a jury trial in **civil cases**, there are some important limits:

- **Cases Not Covered**: The amendment specifically applies to **suits at common law**, not to cases governed by equity or admiralty law. In equity cases, where remedies like injunctions (orders to do or stop doing something) are sought, the courts may resolve disputes without a jury.

- **Judicial Reexamination of Facts**: The second part of the Seventh Amendment prevents a judge from reexamining facts decided by a jury. Once a jury has determined the facts of a case, the judge cannot change that decision unless it violates clear legal principles. This ensures that jury decisions are final and not subject to further review, reinforcing the independence of the jury system.

While the Seventh Amendment was particularly important in the early days of the Republic, today it applies primarily in **federal civil cases**. Most state legal systems provide the right to a jury trial in civil cases as well, but this can vary by state law. The right to a jury trial in civil cases remains a core principle of U.S. law, balancing the judicial process and providing citizens with the ability to influence the outcomes of legal disputes.

The Seventh Amendment ensures that individuals have the right to a jury trial in civil cases, preserving an important principle of justice that allows ordinary citizens to participate in legal decisions. By guaranteeing this right, the amendment provides a check on the power of judges and government, ensuring that justice is not only delivered by the courts but also by the collective judgment of the people.

Amendment VIII: Punishment and Proportionality

The **Eighth Amendment** of the U.S. Constitution is a critical protection against **cruel and unusual punishment** and ensures that penalties for crimes are **proportional** to the offense committed. It aims to ensure that the government does not impose excessive or barbaric punishments, whether physical or otherwise. This amendment protects individuals from punishment that is deemed excessive, inhumane, or degrading.

The Text of the Eighth Amendment

The text of the Eighth Amendment reads:

"Excessive bail shall not be required, nor excessive fines imposed, nor cruel and unusual punishments inflicted."

This short but powerful provision touches on several critical aspects of the criminal justice system, including bail, fines, and punishment. It envisions a justice system where penalties are fair, humane, and aligned with societal standards of decency.

Protection Against Excessive Bail

The Eighth Amendment begins by addressing the issue of **excessive bail**. Bail is the money or property a defendant must provide to be released from jail while awaiting trial, ensuring they appear in court. The amendment protects individuals from being subjected to bail amounts that are

99

unreasonably high or set beyond what is necessary to guarantee the defendant's appearance in court.

- **Fair Bail**: Excessive bail is prohibited, ensuring that individuals are not unjustly imprisoned before their trial due to an inability to pay. This helps maintain the principle that individuals are presumed innocent until proven guilty and prevents them from suffering unnecessarily before their trial.

- **Application in Practice**: In practice, courts must balance the amount of bail with factors such as the severity of the offense, the likelihood that the defendant will appear for trial, and the risk they pose to public safety. The Eighth Amendment ensures that bail is not used as a tool of punishment but as a mechanism to ensure the defendant's appearance in court.

Protection Against Excessive Fines

The second clause of the Eighth Amendment prohibits the imposition of **excessive fines**. Fines are monetary penalties imposed as punishment for a crime or offense, and they are commonly used in both criminal and civil cases. This protection ensures that the amount of a fine is not disproportionately large in relation to the offense committed.

- **Proportionality of Fines**: Just as the Eighth Amendment protects individuals from excessive punishment, it ensures that financial penalties imposed by the government are reasonable and just. The amendment prevents the government from using fines as a form of economic harassment or as a method to impose punishment that is too severe for the offense.

Protection Against Cruel and Unusual Punishment

The most widely discussed aspect of the Eighth Amendment is the prohibition of **cruel and unusual punishment**. This provision aims to prevent the government from inflicting punishments that are deemed inhumane or degrading, reflecting societal standards of decency and fairness.

- **Historical Context**: When the amendment was written, the framers were responding to the brutal punishments that were often used in England, such as torture, public humiliation, and executions. The concept of "cruel and unusual punishment" has evolved over time, but it continues to serve as a critical check on the justice system.

- **Evolving Standards**: The definition of what constitutes "cruel and unusual punishment" has evolved through judicial interpretation, with the Supreme Court making important decisions that reflect changes in societal views on what is acceptable. For example, practices such as **torture** and **public execution** have been outlawed. Additionally, the Court has ruled that **mandatory death sentences** and the execution of **juveniles** or those who are **intellectually disabled** are cruel and unusual.

- **Proportionality of Punishment**: The principle of proportionality is embedded in the Eighth

Amendment. The punishment must fit the crime—what may be appropriate for one offense might be considered excessive or cruel for another. The Supreme Court has used this principle in various cases to assess whether the severity of a sentence or punishment is consistent with the gravity of the crime committed.

The Eighth Amendment is a cornerstone of the U.S. criminal justice system, ensuring that punishments for crimes are fair, just, and humane. It protects individuals from excessive bail, excessive fines, and cruel and unusual punishment, emphasizing the principle that penalties should be proportional to the crime committed. The Eighth Amendment safeguards human dignity and ensures that punishment is not arbitrary, excessive, or degrading, reflecting the values of justice and decency that are fundamental to American law.

Amendment IX: Rights Retained by the People

The **Ninth Amendment** of the U.S. Constitution is often regarded as a safeguard for individual rights that are not specifically enumerated in the Constitution. This amendment addresses the concern that the enumeration of certain rights in the Bill of Rights might lead to the assumption that these are the only rights protected by the Constitution. The Ninth Amendment explicitly states that the **people's rights are not limited to those listed in the Constitution**. Its text reads:

"The enumeration in the Constitution, of certain rights, shall not be construed to deny or disparage others retained by the people."

The Purpose and Intent of the Ninth Amendment

The Ninth Amendment was added to address the concerns of those who believed that by listing specific rights (such as freedom of speech, the right to bear arms, and protection against unreasonable searches), the framers of the Constitution might inadvertently imply that any rights not explicitly mentioned were not protected.

- **A Broad View of Rights**: The Ninth Amendment makes it clear that just because a right is not specifically mentioned in the Constitution does not mean it is not protected. This provides a broad safeguard for individual liberties, emphasizing that the people have many rights that exist beyond those enumerated in the Constitution. The framers intended for this amendment to preserve the idea that rights come from natural law or inherent human dignity, rather than being granted solely by the government.

- **Interpretation of Unenumerated Rights**: Over time, the Ninth Amendment has been used by courts to recognize rights that are not specifically listed in the Constitution. One of the most significant examples of this is the **right to privacy**, which, though not explicitly mentioned in the text of the Constitution, was recognized by the Supreme Court in cases like **Griswold v. Connecticut** (1965) and later in **Roe v. Wade** (1973). The Ninth Amendment provides a constitutional basis for the idea that citizens possess certain rights that are fundamental to their liberty, even if they are not listed in the Bill of Rights.

Implications for Judicial Interpretation

While the Ninth Amendment itself does not specify which rights are protected, it plays an essential role in the judicial interpretation of rights. It helps ensure that constitutional protections evolve with time, allowing courts to recognize and safeguard new or emerging rights that may not have been foreseen by the framers but are consistent with the spirit of individual liberty.

- **Protection of Fundamental Freedoms**: The Ninth Amendment supports a living interpretation of the Constitution that adapts to changing social, political, and technological conditions. It guarantees that as society develops, the recognition of rights will not be limited to those explicitly mentioned in the document.

- **Limiting Government Overreach**: This amendment also serves as a reminder that the government cannot infringe upon unenumerated rights simply because they are not written down. The government must still respect the broader principle of individual liberty and freedom, even when certain rights are not explicitly stated.

The Ninth Amendment serves as an important safeguard for individual freedoms, ensuring that the listing of specific rights in the Bill of Rights does not exclude other rights that the people retain. It is a vital piece of the constitutional framework, supporting a broader understanding of personal liberty and helping to ensure that the Constitution remains adaptable to the evolving needs of the nation.

Amendment X: Powers Reserved to the States and the People

The **Tenth Amendment** of the U.S. Constitution is a critical component of the **federalism** structure that defines the relationship between the national government and the state governments. It reaffirms the principle that any powers not specifically granted to the federal government by the Constitution are reserved for the **states** or the **people**. The text of the Tenth Amendment reads:

"The powers not delegated to the United States by the Constitution, nor prohibited by it to the States, are reserved to the States respectively, or to the people."

The Principle of Federalism

The Tenth Amendment was included to clarify the distribution of powers between the federal government and the state governments. The framers of the Constitution were deeply committed to the idea of **federalism**, which divides governmental authority between the national government and the individual states. This division ensures that power is not concentrated in one central authority, but is instead shared between multiple levels of government.

- **Limits on Federal Power**: The Tenth Amendment is a limitation on the powers of the federal government. It ensures that any powers not explicitly granted to the federal government by the Constitution, nor prohibited to the states, remain within the authority of the states or the people. This provision was particularly important to those who feared that the new Constitution would create a central government with unchecked power.

- **Reserved Powers**: The Tenth Amendment embodies the principle that the federal government only has the powers specifically enumerated in the Constitution. If a power is not granted to the federal government, it belongs either to the states or to the people, giving the states significant authority to govern and regulate matters within their own borders.

State Sovereignty and Individual Liberties

The Tenth Amendment supports **state sovereignty**, which ensures that states have the ability to legislate and govern in areas not controlled by the federal government. It allows states to exercise a range of powers, including the regulation of **education, criminal justice, healthcare, marriage**, and **local business practices**, among others. This decentralization of power allows states to address the unique needs and preferences of their citizens.

- **Balancing National and State Interests**: The Tenth Amendment helps preserve the balance between national and state interests, ensuring that states maintain significant autonomy in areas that are not within the federal government's purview. While the federal government has authority over issues that affect the entire nation (such as national defense, foreign policy, and interstate commerce), the Tenth

Amendment ensures that states retain broad authority over matters that are more localized.

- **Empowering the People**: The Tenth Amendment also reserves powers to the **people**, which reinforces the idea that ultimate sovereignty rests with the citizens themselves. When state governments or the federal government act outside their constitutional authority, the people have the right to challenge such actions through voting, civil action, or legal means.

The Tenth Amendment and Supreme Court Interpretations

Over time, the **Supreme Court** has interpreted the Tenth Amendment in various ways, often in the context of cases involving the division of power between federal and state governments.

- **Expanded Federal Power**: In some cases, the Court has interpreted the Constitution in a way that grants broader power to the federal government, particularly in areas such as commerce and national defense. For example, under the **Commerce Clause** (Article I, Section 8), Congress has been granted the authority to regulate interstate commerce, which has allowed the federal government to exert significant influence over the states in certain areas.

- **States' Rights**: In other cases, the Tenth Amendment has been cited in support of state authority, especially when state powers were being infringed upon by the federal government. For instance, in cases involving state regulation of business practices or local law enforcement, the Court has occasionally ruled in favor of preserving state authority.

The Tenth Amendment is a fundamental part of the Constitution's framework of **federalism**. It ensures that powers not specifically granted to the federal government are reserved to the states or the people, maintaining a balance of power that prevents federal overreach and preserves state sovereignty. It is a reminder of the Constitution's commitment to limiting government power and preserving individual freedoms, allowing states and local communities to govern themselves in areas not expressly covered by federal law.

Together with the other amendments in the Bill of Rights, the Tenth Amendment is vital to maintaining the constitutional system of government and protecting the rights of citizens from encroachment by either the federal government or the states.

Part V: Amendments That Reshaped the Nation

The Eleventh and Twelfth Amendments were significant changes that helped define the functioning of the U.S. government, particularly in the areas of judicial power and the presidential election process. These amendments address practical issues that emerged after the nation's early years, adapting the Constitution to new realities and ensuring that the government operates efficiently and fairly.

Amendment XI: Limits on Judicial Power (1795)

The **Eleventh Amendment** was passed in response to the **Supreme Court's decision in Chisholm v. Georgia (1793)**, in which the Court ruled that a citizen of one state could sue another state in federal court. This decision was seen as a potential threat to state sovereignty, leading to concerns that states could be sued by individuals from other states or even foreign nations. In response, the **Eleventh Amendment** was enacted to limit the jurisdiction of federal courts.

The text of the **Eleventh Amendment** reads:

"The Judicial power of the United States shall not be construed to extend to any suit in law or equity, commenced or prosecuted against one of the United States by Citizens

110

of another State, or by Citizens or Subjects of any Foreign State."

Key Provisions of Amendment XI

- **Sovereign Immunity**: The amendment establishes the principle of **sovereign immunity**, meaning that states cannot be sued in federal court by citizens of other states or foreign nationals without their consent. This was intended to protect state sovereignty and prevent federal courts from being used to challenge state laws or policies.

- **Limits on Federal Court Jurisdiction**: The Eleventh Amendment clarifies the boundaries of federal judicial authority, preventing federal courts from hearing cases where a state is sued by an out-of-state citizen or a foreign entity. This provides a greater degree of autonomy to states, ensuring that they are not subject to lawsuits from individuals outside their jurisdiction.

- **Impact on State Sovereignty**: The amendment reinforced the idea that states retain significant powers under the Constitution, preserving their autonomy and protecting them from potentially disruptive legal challenges brought in federal courts.

Amendment XII: Presidential Election Procedures (1804)

The **Twelfth Amendment** was introduced to reform the process by which the President and Vice President were elected, a system that had become problematic in practice.

Under the original design of the **Constitution**, members of the Electoral College cast two votes for President, and the candidate with the most votes became President, while the runner-up became Vice President. This process led to confusion and conflict, particularly in the election of **1800**, which resulted in a tie between Thomas Jefferson and Aaron Burr.

The text of the **Twelfth Amendment** reads:

"The Electors shall meet in their respective States and vote by Ballot for President and Vice President, one of whom, at least, shall not be an inhabitant of the same State with themselves."

Key Provisions of Amendment XII

- **Separate Ballots for President and Vice President**: The most important change introduced by the Twelfth Amendment was the requirement for electors to cast separate votes for **President** and **Vice President**. This ensured that the President and Vice President would not be political rivals from the same party, as had happened in **1800** when Jefferson and Burr tied, creating confusion and a political crisis.

- **Clarification of Electoral College Procedure**: The amendment also clarified the procedure for electing the President and Vice President, specifying that if no candidate receives a majority of the Electoral College votes, the election would be decided by the **House of Representatives** for the President and by the **Senate** for the Vice President. This was designed to streamline the process and reduce the risk of a deadlock.

- **Political Parties and Running Mates**: While the Constitution originally assumed that the President and Vice President might come from different parties, the Twelfth Amendment indirectly acknowledged the rise of political parties by ensuring that the President and Vice President were elected as a team. This amendment laid the foundation for the modern system of political parties in American elections.

Amendments 11 and 12 helped adapt the Constitution to the evolving political landscape. The Eleventh Amendment strengthened state sovereignty by limiting the power of federal courts over state matters, and the Twelfth Amendment addressed flaws in the presidential election system, creating the framework for the modern process of electing a President and Vice President. Both amendments helped stabilize and streamline governance during a time of growing national complexity.

Amendments 13–15: Ending Slavery and Expanding Citizenship

The **Thirteenth, Fourteenth**, and **Fifteenth Amendments**, collectively known as the **Reconstruction Amendments**, were passed in the aftermath of the Civil War. These three amendments fundamentally reshaped the U.S. legal and political landscape, addressing the issues of slavery, citizenship, and voting rights. They sought to secure the rights of newly freed African Americans and guarantee their equality under the law.

Amendment XIII: Abolition of Slavery (1865)

The **Thirteenth Amendment** was a landmark change in American history, abolishing **slavery and involuntary servitude** in the United States. It was passed after the Civil War and was a crucial step toward fulfilling the promise of liberty and equality for all Americans, particularly African Americans.

The text of the **Thirteenth Amendment** reads:

"Neither slavery nor involuntary servitude, except as a punishment for crime whereof the party shall have been duly convicted, shall exist within the United States, or any place subject to their jurisdiction."

Key Provisions of Amendment XIII

- **Abolition of Slavery**: The amendment makes it unconstitutional to own slaves in the United States. It freed all enslaved individuals and formally ended

114

the practice of slavery, which had been a significant issue in American history, particularly in the Southern states.

- **Punishment Exception**: The only exception allowed under the amendment is for individuals who have been convicted of a crime. In such cases, individuals may be forced to work as part of their punishment, though this has led to debates over **prison labor** and **forced labor in the criminal justice system**.

Amendment XIV: Citizenship and Equal Protection (1868)

The **Fourteenth Amendment** is one of the most important amendments in American history, as it guarantees **equal protection under the law** and **due process** for all citizens. It was created to ensure that the rights of African Americans were protected following the Civil War and to extend the full protections of the Bill of Rights to all citizens, regardless of state laws.

The text of the **Fourteenth Amendment** reads:

"All persons born or naturalized in the United States, and subject to the jurisdiction thereof, are citizens of the United States and of the State wherein they reside."

Key Provisions of Amendment XIV

- **Citizenship Clause**: The Fourteenth Amendment grants **citizenship** to all persons born or naturalized in the United States, including formerly enslaved people. This overturned the Supreme Court's **Dred**

Scott v. Sandford decision (1857), which held that African Americans could not be citizens.

- **Due Process Clause**: The amendment provides that no state can deprive any person of life, liberty, or property without **due process of law**. This ensures that state governments must respect individual rights and follow fair legal procedures.

- **Equal Protection Clause**: The amendment guarantees that no state shall deny any person within its jurisdiction **equal protection of the laws**. This is a powerful tool for fighting discrimination and has been the basis for numerous landmark rulings on civil rights issues.

Amendment XV: Voting Rights (1870)

The **Fifteenth Amendment** furthered the goals of the Reconstruction Amendments by **guaranteeing voting rights** for all male citizens, regardless of race, color, or previous condition of servitude. This was a critical step in ensuring political equality for African Americans.

The text of the **Fifteenth Amendment** reads:

"The right of citizens of the United States to vote shall not be denied or abridged by the United States or by any State on account of race, color, or previous condition of servitude."

Key Provisions of Amendment XV

- **Voting Rights for All Men**: The Fifteenth Amendment prohibited states from denying the vote based on race, color, or prior enslavement. It aimed to ensure that African American men could participate fully in the political process.

- **Limitations and Challenges**: While the Fifteenth Amendment was a monumental victory, its full realization was impeded by practices like **poll taxes**, **literacy tests**, and **grandfather clauses** in Southern states, which were designed to disenfranchise African American voters. It was only through later civil rights legislation, including the **Voting Rights Act of 1965**, that these discriminatory practices were significantly challenged and curtailed.

The **Reconstruction Amendments**—the Thirteenth, Fourteenth, and Fifteenth Amendments—were pivotal in reshaping the nation after the Civil War. They abolished slavery, guaranteed citizenship and equal protection under the law, and sought to ensure that African Americans had the right to vote. These amendments were instrumental in laying the groundwork for future civil rights movements and legal challenges, advancing the cause of racial equality in the United States.

Amendments 16–19: Taxes, Democracy, and Women's Suffrage

The **Sixteenth, Seventeenth, Eighteenth,** and **Nineteenth Amendments** represent significant shifts in American governance, focusing on taxation, the expansion of democratic participation, and the recognition of women's rights. These amendments reflect the evolving social and political landscape of the United States during the late 19th and early 20th centuries. They address the changing needs of an industrialized nation and mark the progression of civil rights.

Amendment XVI: Income Tax (1913)

The **Sixteenth Amendment** grants Congress the power to impose and collect **income taxes** without apportioning them among the states or basing them on population. This amendment was passed in response to concerns that the federal government needed a more stable revenue source to fund its growing responsibilities.

The text of the **Sixteenth Amendment** reads:

"The Congress shall have power to lay and collect taxes on incomes, from whatever source derived, without apportionment among the several States, and without regard to any census or enumeration."

Key Provisions of Amendment XVI

- **Power to Tax Income**: Prior to the Sixteenth Amendment, income taxes were subject to the apportionment requirement, which limited their scope. The amendment removed this limitation, giving Congress the ability to levy income taxes directly, regardless of state populations. This change provided the federal government with a significant and consistent source of revenue.

- **Revenue for Federal Government**: The ability to collect income taxes allowed the federal government to fund large-scale projects, including **infrastructure**, **social programs**, and **military needs**. It also enabled the government to address the economic challenges posed by industrialization, urbanization, and the increasing complexity of the national economy.

Amendment XVII: Direct Election of Senators (1913)

The **Seventeenth Amendment** was passed to change the method of selecting U.S. Senators, shifting the process from selection by state legislatures to direct election by the people. This amendment aimed to make the Senate more democratic and responsive to the public will.

The text of the **Seventeenth Amendment** reads:

"The Senate of the United States shall be composed of two Senators from each State, chosen by the people thereof; for six years; and each Senator shall have one vote."

Key Provisions of Amendment XVII

- **Direct Election of Senators**: Before the Seventeenth Amendment, U.S. Senators were chosen by state legislatures, a system that was often criticized for being undemocratic and subject to corruption. The amendment allows citizens to directly vote for their Senators, increasing public control over the legislative process.

- **Increase in Democratic Participation**: The shift to direct election of Senators expanded democratic participation and reduced the influence of political machines and elite control over the selection of federal legislators. It was part of a broader movement for **political reform** that included **women's suffrage** and **direct primaries**.

Amendment XVIII: Prohibition of Alcohol (1919)

The **Eighteenth Amendment** prohibited the manufacture, sale, and transportation of alcoholic beverages in the United States, initiating the era known as **Prohibition**. This amendment was the result of a decades-long campaign by temperance movements, which argued that alcohol was a destructive influence on society.

The text of the **Eighteenth Amendment** reads:

"After one year from the ratification of this article the manufacture, sale, or transportation of intoxicating liquors...for beverage purposes is hereby prohibited."

Key Provisions of Amendment XVIII

- **Prohibition of Alcohol**: The amendment made it illegal to produce, sell, or transport alcoholic beverages. This was intended to reduce alcohol-related problems such as domestic violence, crime, and public health issues.

- **Rise of Organized Crime**: Despite its good intentions, Prohibition led to unintended consequences. It contributed to the rise of **organized crime** and illegal **bootlegging**, as criminals profited from the illegal trade of alcohol. Public dissatisfaction with Prohibition led to its eventual repeal in 1933 with the **Twenty-First Amendment**.

Amendment XIX: Women's Suffrage (1920)

The **Nineteenth Amendment** was one of the most significant expansions of democratic rights in American history. It granted women the right to vote, marking the culmination of the **women's suffrage movement**, which had been fighting for women's voting rights for over a century.

The text of the **Nineteenth Amendment** reads:

"The right of citizens of the United States to vote shall not be denied or abridged by the United States or by any State on account of sex."

Key Provisions of Amendment XIX

- **Granting Women the Right to Vote**: The amendment granted women full suffrage, ensuring that gender could no longer be a barrier to voting. This was a monumental achievement in the fight for gender equality and was the result of tireless activism by suffragists such as **Susan B. Anthony**, **Elizabeth Cady Stanton**, and **Alice Paul**.

- **Expanding Democracy**: With the passage of the Nineteenth Amendment, American democracy became more inclusive. Women could now participate fully in the democratic process, influencing the nation's political decisions through voting. The amendment not only altered the political landscape but also set the stage for further advances in women's rights and gender equality.

The **Sixteenth, Seventeenth, Eighteenth,** and **Nineteenth Amendments** reshaped the U.S. government in significant ways. They expanded the power of the federal government through the introduction of income taxes, increased democratic participation by allowing for the direct election of Senators and women's suffrage, and led to social and political changes like Prohibition. These amendments reflect the evolving values of American society during a period of rapid change and reform, laying the groundwork for future constitutional developments.

Amendments 20–23: Modern Presidential Government

The **Twentieth**, **Twenty-First**, **Twenty-Second**, and **Twenty-Third Amendments** focus on modernizing the U.S. government's presidential election process, adjusting terms of office, and addressing the electoral rights of Washington, D.C. residents. These amendments respond to the practical needs of a growing nation and help ensure that the presidential and governmental systems function efficiently.

Amendment XX: Presidential Terms and Congressional Sessions (1933)

The **Twentieth Amendment**, also known as the **Lame Duck Amendment**, was passed to address issues related to the terms of office for the President, Vice President, and Congress. It reduced the time between election day and the start of the new presidential term, which previously was too long.

The text of the **Twentieth Amendment** reads:

"The terms of the President and Vice President shall end at noon on the 20th day of January...The Congress shall assemble at least once in every year, and such meeting shall begin at noon on the 3rd day of January..."

Key Provisions of Amendment XX

- **Shortening the Lame Duck Period**: Prior to the Twentieth Amendment, there was a long delay

123

between the election in November and the inauguration of the new President and Congress in March. The Twentieth Amendment moved the presidential inauguration date to **January 20** and the start of Congressional terms to **January 3**, shortening the "lame duck" period and ensuring a quicker transition of power.

- **Clarifying Presidential Succession**: The amendment also clarified the procedures for presidential succession, specifying what happens if the President-elect dies before taking office, further solidifying the continuity of government.

Amendment XXI: Repeal of Prohibition (1933)

The **Twenty-First Amendment** repealed the **Eighteenth Amendment**, effectively ending **Prohibition**. This amendment reversed the previous decision that had made the sale and consumption of alcohol illegal, recognizing the failure of Prohibition and the negative social consequences it had caused.

The text of the **Twenty-First Amendment** reads:

"The eighteenth article of amendment to the Constitution of the United States is hereby repealed."

Key Provisions of Amendment XXI

- **Repealing Prohibition**: The Twenty-First Amendment is unique because it is the only amendment that repeals a previous one. It ended the nationwide ban on alcohol, which had led to widespread illegal activity and was unpopular with large segments of the population.

- **State Control Over Alcohol Regulation**: The amendment allowed individual states to regulate alcohol laws within their borders, providing a more flexible and practical system of control.

Amendment XXII: Presidential Term Limits (1951)

The **Twenty-Second Amendment** limits the number of terms a President can serve to two, or a total of ten years if they assume office in the middle of a term.

The text of the **Twenty-Second Amendment** reads:

"No person shall be elected to the office of the President more than twice..."

Key Provisions of Amendment XXII

- **Limiting Presidential Power**: The amendment was passed after the unprecedented four terms served by **Franklin D. Roosevelt**, whose leadership during the Great Depression and World War II raised concerns about the concentration of power in one individual. The amendment ensures that no President can hold office indefinitely, thereby preventing a potential **dictatorship**.

- **Promoting Democratic Change**: By limiting the President to two terms, the amendment promotes democratic turnover and ensures that new leadership can emerge, preventing any one individual from becoming too entrenched in power.

Amendment XXIII: Electoral Votes for Washington, D.C. (1961)

The **Twenty-Third Amendment** grants **residents of Washington, D.C.** the right to vote in presidential elections by awarding them **electoral votes** in the **Electoral College**. Before this amendment, D.C. residents were not allowed to participate in presidential elections.

The text of the **Twenty-Third Amendment** reads:

"The District constituting the seat of Government of the United States shall appoint in such manner as the Congress may direct: a number of electors of President and Vice President equal to the whole number of Senators and Representatives in Congress to which the District would be entitled if it were a State..."

Key Provisions of Amendment XXIII

- **Representation in Presidential Elections**: The amendment gives D.C. residents the right to vote for President and Vice President, ensuring that they have a voice in the presidential election, just as citizens of the states do.

- **No Congressional Representation**: While D.C. residents gained the right to vote in presidential elections, they still do not have voting representation in Congress. The amendment did not grant D.C. full statehood or congressional representation, which remains a topic of debate.

The **Twentieth, Twenty-First, Twenty-Second**, and **Twenty-Third Amendments** reflect the evolution of U.S.

governance in the modern era. They address issues related to presidential succession, the repeal of Prohibition, the limitation of presidential power, and the electoral rights of D.C. residents. These amendments are part of the broader effort to ensure that the U.S. government remains responsive to the needs of a changing society while maintaining democratic principles.

Amendments 24–26: Voting Rights Expanded

The **Twenty-Fourth**, **Twenty-Fifth**, and **Twenty-Sixth Amendments** represent significant expansions of voting rights and democratic participation in the United States. These amendments reflect the nation's ongoing efforts to ensure that every eligible citizen has an equal opportunity to participate in the electoral process.

Amendment XXIV: Abolition of Poll Taxes (1964)

The **Twenty-Fourth Amendment** was passed to abolish **poll taxes** in federal elections. Poll taxes were fees that voters had to pay in order to cast a ballot, and they were used in several Southern states as a means to disenfranchise African American voters and other marginalized groups, particularly during the era of **Jim Crow laws**.

The text of the **Twenty-Fourth Amendment** reads:

"The right of citizens of the United States to vote in any primary or other election for President, Vice President, electors for President or Vice President, or for Senator or Representative in Congress, shall not be denied or abridged by the United States or by any State by reason of failure to pay any poll tax or other tax."

Key Provisions of Amendment XXIV

- **Elimination of Poll Taxes**: The amendment made it unconstitutional for any state or local government to impose a poll tax on voters in federal elections. This significantly reduced barriers to voting for lower-income citizens, who were often disproportionately affected by such taxes.

- **Protection of Voting Rights**: By eliminating poll taxes, the amendment was an important step toward protecting the right to vote as a fundamental American right. It also helped ensure that economic status would no longer be used as a tool of voter suppression.

Amendment XXV: Presidential Disability and Succession (1967)

The **Twenty-Fifth Amendment** clarified the procedures for presidential **disability** and **succession**. This amendment was introduced following concerns about the potential incapacitation of the president, particularly after the **assassination of President John F. Kennedy** in 1963, which raised questions about presidential continuity and the transfer of power.

The text of the **Twenty-Fifth Amendment** reads:

"In case of the removal of the President from office or of his death or resignation, the Vice President shall become President. Whenever there is a vacancy in the office of the Vice President, the President shall nominate a Vice President who shall take office upon confirmation by a majority vote of both Houses of Congress."

Key Provisions of Amendment XXV

- **Presidential Succession**: The amendment ensures that if the President dies, resigns, or is removed from office, the **Vice President** becomes President. This was an important clarification, as the Constitution had been vague on the procedures for presidential succession.

- **Presidential Disability**: The amendment also provides a clear procedure for situations in which the President is unable to perform their duties due to illness or incapacity. If the President is unable to fulfill their role, the Vice President can assume the powers of the presidency temporarily.

- **Vacancy in the Vice Presidency**: The amendment also addressed what happens if the Vice President's office becomes vacant. It allows the President to nominate a new Vice President, who must be confirmed by a majority vote of both houses of Congress. This ensures that the line of succession remains intact.

Amendment XXVI: Lowering the Voting Age to 18 (1971)

The **Twenty-Sixth Amendment** lowered the **voting age** from 21 to 18. This change was driven by the **Vietnam War**, during which young Americans were drafted to serve in the military but were not able to vote on the policies that affected their lives and futures.

The text of the **Twenty-Sixth Amendment** reads:

"The right of citizens of the United States, who are eighteen years of age or older, to vote shall not be denied or abridged by the United States or by any State on account of age."

Key Provisions of Amendment XXVI

- **Lowering the Voting Age**: The amendment granted **18-year-olds** the right to vote in all federal, state, and local elections, reflecting the belief that if young people were old enough to fight and die in wars, they should also be trusted to vote.

- **Expansion of Democracy**: The amendment expanded the electorate significantly, granting millions of young Americans the right to participate in the democratic process. This helped increase the representation of younger generations in elections, giving them a stronger voice in shaping government policy.

The **Twenty-Fourth**, **Twenty-Fifth**, and **Twenty-Sixth Amendments** represent significant milestones in the expansion of voting rights and the protection of democratic principles. By abolishing poll taxes, clarifying presidential succession and disability, and lowering the voting age, these amendments strengthened the democratic system and made it more inclusive, ensuring that more citizens could participate in the electoral process and that the mechanisms of government could function smoothly in times of crisis or transition.

Amendment 27: Congressional Pay (1992)

The **Twenty-Seventh Amendment** deals with the issue of **congressional pay**, ensuring that any changes to the compensation of members of Congress cannot take effect until after the next election. This amendment was first proposed in 1789, but it was not ratified until 1992, making it one of the longest ratification processes in American history.

The text of the **Twenty-Seventh Amendment** reads:

"No law, varying the compensation for the services of the Senators and Representatives, shall take effect, until an election of Representatives shall have intervened."

Key Provisions of Amendment 27

- **Limits on Congressional Pay Increases**: The amendment prevents members of Congress from giving themselves immediate pay raises. If Congress passes a law that changes their compensation, the change will not take effect until after the next election for the House of Representatives. This ensures that lawmakers cannot vote themselves a pay raise without the electorate having the opportunity to weigh in on their decision in the next election.

- **Prevention of Self-Dealing**: The amendment was designed to prevent potential abuses of power and ensure that elected officials are held accountable for their decisions regarding their own pay. By delaying the impact of pay changes, the amendment reinforces the idea that members of Congress should be responsive to the public and should not be able to unilaterally adjust their compensation.

- **Historical Context and Delayed Ratification**: The amendment was originally proposed as part of the **original Bill of Rights** in 1789 but was not ratified until 1992, making it the most recent amendment to the Constitution. Its passage came after a public outcry over congressional pay raises in the late 1980s and early 1990s, and it reflects the continued importance of ensuring that Congress remains accountable to the people.

The **Twenty-Seventh Amendment** ensures that changes to congressional pay are made with careful consideration and only after the electorate has had the opportunity to vote in the next congressional election. It serves as an important check on the power of legislators to control their own compensation, promoting transparency and accountability in government. Despite its long and delayed ratification, it highlights the ongoing relevance of public scrutiny in the legislative process.

Part VI: Your Rights in Everyday Life

Your Rights When Dealing With Police

Interactions with law enforcement can be stressful and intimidating, but it's essential to know your rights to protect yourself and ensure that your interactions are fair and lawful. The U.S. Constitution, through various amendments, provides critical protections when dealing with the police, particularly the **Fourth, Fifth, Sixth**, and **Eighth Amendments**.

The Right to Remain Silent (Fifth Amendment)

One of your most important rights when dealing with police is the **right to remain silent**. Under the **Fifth Amendment**, you are not obligated to speak to law enforcement officers during an encounter. This right is critical, especially during questioning or when arrested.

- **Miranda Rights**: When you are placed under arrest, the police are required to inform you of your right to remain silent and your right to an attorney. These rights are known as **Miranda rights**, and the police must read them to you before any interrogation. If they fail to do so, anything you say cannot be used against you in court.

- **Refusing to Answer Questions**: If the police stop you or question you, you have the right to refuse to answer questions. You can simply state, "I am exercising my right to remain silent." However, you should also be cooperative in terms of providing basic identification (e.g., your name) if requested.

The Right to Be Free from Unreasonable Searches and Seizures (Fourth Amendment)

The **Fourth Amendment** protects you from unreasonable searches and seizures. This means that the police generally cannot search your body, home, car, or belongings without a **warrant** or **probable cause**.

- **Search Warrant**: A search warrant is a legal document authorized by a judge, permitting the police to search a specific location and seize evidence. If the police do not have a warrant, they must have probable cause to search you or your property.

- **Exceptions to Warrant Requirement**: There are exceptions to the warrant requirement, such as:

  o **Consent Searches**: If you consent to a search, the police can search you or your property without a warrant. However, you are free to decline the search.

  o **Searches Incident to Arrest**: If you are arrested, the police can search you and the area within your immediate control to ensure officer safety and to prevent destruction of evidence.

  o **Exigent Circumstances**: If there is an urgent situation (e.g., a threat to life or the imminent destruction of evidence), the police can search without a warrant.

- **The Right to Challenge Unlawful Searches**: If the police violate your Fourth Amendment rights during a search, the evidence gathered from that search may be inadmissible in court (the **exclusionary rule**).

The Right to Be Free From Self-Incrimination (Fifth Amendment)

Under the **Fifth Amendment**, you have the right not to incriminate yourself. This means that during an arrest or detention, you do not have to provide information that could be used against you in a criminal case.

- **Interrogation**: You cannot be forced to make self-incriminating statements during questioning. If the police attempt to question you after an arrest, you have the right to remain silent.

- **Invoking Your Rights**: If you are being questioned by police and wish to exercise your right to remain silent, simply state, "I am invoking my right to remain silent" or "I wish to speak with an attorney." From that point, the police should stop questioning you until your lawyer is present.

Your Right to an Attorney (Sixth Amendment)

If you are arrested or detained, you have the right to **legal counsel** under the **Sixth Amendment**. This right ensures that you can have an attorney present to guide you through legal processes and protect your rights.

- **Right to Legal Representation**: If you cannot afford an attorney, one will be provided to you at no cost (this is known as a **public defender**).

- **Right to Have an Attorney Present During Interrogation**: If you are being questioned, you can request an attorney. Once you request an attorney, the police are required to stop questioning you until your attorney is present.

The Right to Be Free from Cruel and Unusual Punishment (Eighth Amendment)

The **Eighth Amendment** prohibits cruel and unusual punishment. This means that during an arrest or detention, law enforcement officers are not allowed to use excessive force or subject you to degrading or inhumane treatment.

- **Excessive Force**: If police use excessive force or abuse their power while arresting or detaining you, you may have grounds to file a complaint or a lawsuit. You should document the incident and seek legal counsel if necessary.

- **Right to Humane Treatment**: Even after an arrest, you are entitled to humane treatment in detention, including adequate food, water, and access to medical care if needed.

What to Do If Your Rights Are Violated

If you believe your rights have been violated during an encounter with the police, it's essential to stay calm and keep a record of the events. If possible, take note of the officers' names and badge numbers, and gather witness testimony. File a complaint with the local police department or seek legal assistance to challenge any wrongful actions taken by law enforcement.

Conclusion of Your Rights When Dealing with Police

Understanding your rights when interacting with law enforcement is crucial for protecting yourself and ensuring that the legal system respects your constitutional protections. Knowing your **rights to remain silent, right to be free from unreasonable searches**, and **right to legal representation** can help you navigate these interactions with confidence and awareness.

Your Rights in Court

When you are involved in legal proceedings, whether as a defendant, plaintiff, or witness, your rights in court are fundamental to ensuring a fair trial and the protection of your constitutional liberties. The **Sixth, Seventh, Eighth,** and **Fourteenth Amendments** provide key protections that govern your treatment in the courtroom.

The Right to a Speedy and Public Trial (Sixth Amendment)

The **Sixth Amendment** guarantees the right to a **speedy and public trial** by an impartial jury. This ensures that you are not held indefinitely or subjected to unreasonable delays before having your day in court.

- **Speedy Trial**: The amendment prevents the government from holding you in jail for extended periods without trial. If you are accused of a crime, the trial must begin within a reasonable time frame, ensuring that justice is timely and not delayed by unnecessary bureaucratic processes.

- **Public Trial**: Trials must be open to the public to maintain transparency and accountability in the judicial process. This helps prevent unfair trials and ensures that the public can observe the administration of justice.

The Right to an Impartial Jury (Sixth Amendment)

You are entitled to a trial by an **impartial jury** of your peers. This means that the jurors must not have a bias or preconceived notions about your case.

- **Jury of Your Peers**: The jury should represent a cross-section of the community, providing a fair and unbiased verdict. Jurors are selected through a process known as **voir dire**, where both the defense and prosecution can question potential jurors to determine if they are fit to serve.

- **Challenges to Jurors**: If you believe that a juror cannot be impartial, you or your attorney can challenge their inclusion in the jury.

The Right to Be Informed of the Charges Against You (Sixth Amendment)

The Sixth Amendment also guarantees the right to be informed of the **nature and cause of the accusation** against you. This means that you must be clearly informed of the charges you are facing so you can prepare a defense.

- **Notice of Charges**: If you are arrested, the police must inform you of the charges against you. In court, the prosecution must present evidence and make its case so you can understand the accusations and have the opportunity to challenge them.

The Right to Confront Witnesses (Sixth Amendment)

The Sixth Amendment grants you the right to **confront and cross-examine** witnesses who testify against you in court.

- **Cross-Examination**: You or your attorney have the right to question the prosecution's witnesses. This ensures that you have an opportunity to challenge the credibility and reliability of the evidence presented against you.

- **Witness Testimony**: You also have the right to present witnesses on your behalf and compel them to testify in your favor.

The Right to Legal Counsel (Sixth Amendment)

The Sixth Amendment guarantees that you have the **right to counsel** (an attorney) during criminal prosecutions. If you cannot afford an attorney, one will be appointed for you.

- **Right to an Attorney**: Having legal representation ensures that you have someone to guide you through the complexities of the legal system and advocate for your rights. The government is obligated to provide counsel if you cannot afford an attorney.

The Right to Be Free from Cruel and Unusual Punishment (Eighth Amendment)

The **Eighth Amendment** protects you from **cruel and unusual punishment** in court, ensuring that the penalties imposed for a crime are not excessively harsh or inhumane.

- **Fair Sentencing**: If convicted, the punishment must be proportional to the crime. The amendment prohibits torture or degrading punishment and ensures that sentences are fair and appropriate for the offense.

The Right to Appeal (Due Process)

The **Fourteenth Amendment** guarantees **due process** rights, meaning that any criminal proceeding must be conducted fairly, and any verdict reached must be in accordance with the law. If you are found guilty in a trial, you have the right to **appeal** the decision to a higher court if you believe there was an error in your case.

- **Appeals**: If you think your trial was unfair or the law was incorrectly applied, you have the right to request that a higher court review the case.

Your rights in court ensure that the legal process is fair and just. The **right to a speedy and public trial**, **right to an impartial jury**, and **right to counsel** are critical safeguards that protect you from injustice. Knowing these rights helps ensure that you are treated fairly in the legal system, whether you are a defendant, a plaintiff, or a witness.

Your Rights to Speak, Protest, and Organize

The **First Amendment** to the U.S. Constitution protects some of the most fundamental freedoms that form the bedrock of American democracy: **freedom of speech, freedom of the press, freedom of assembly, freedom of religion**, and the **right to petition the government**. These rights are essential for individuals to express their views, challenge authority, and work collectively to bring about change.

Freedom of Speech

The **First Amendment** guarantees the right to **freedom of speech**, meaning you can express your ideas and opinions freely without government interference or censorship. This protection extends to all forms of communication, including spoken words, written material, symbolic speech (like protests or wearing symbols), and even online platforms.

- **Limitations on Free Speech**: While the First Amendment provides broad protections, it is not absolute. The government can place certain limits on speech if it poses a clear and present danger, incites violence, or defames others. For example, **hate speech, incitement to violence**, and **libel** (false written statements that damage someone's reputation) are not protected by the First Amendment.

- **Political Speech**: Political speech, in particular, is highly protected. The **Supreme Court** has consistently upheld the right to express political opinions, whether through speech, writing, or public demonstrations. This allows individuals to criticize the government, protest against laws, and advocate for change.

Freedom of Assembly and Protest

The **right to assemble** is another crucial protection under the First Amendment. It guarantees the right to come together with others in public spaces to express your views, rally for a cause, and engage in collective action.

- **Peaceful Protest**: The First Amendment protects peaceful protest as a form of expressing dissent against government policies or societal issues. The right to protest is vital for social movements, allowing citizens to publicly challenge authority and bring attention to injustices. However, it is important to note that the right to assemble is generally limited to peaceful protests. **Violent protests** or actions that disrupt public order can be subject to legal restrictions.

- **Permits for Protests**: While you have the right to protest, some local governments may require permits for large gatherings, especially if they are held in public spaces or on private property. These permits are meant to ensure public safety and to allow for proper planning, but they cannot be used to prevent protest based on the content of the speech.

The Right to Petition the Government

The First Amendment also guarantees the **right to petition the government** for a redress of grievances. This means that you have the right to express your concerns or request changes to policies or laws without fear of retaliation.

- **Petitioning**: This can take many forms, including writing letters to elected officials, organizing petitions, filing complaints, and even engaging in public campaigns or lobbying efforts. The right to petition empowers citizens to seek governmental action or address perceived wrongs.

Freedom of the Press

The **freedom of the press** is a critical protection for journalists and media outlets, ensuring they can operate without government interference. The press plays an essential role in informing the public, exposing corruption, and holding the government accountable.

- **Investigative Journalism**: Journalists can investigate government actions, corporate wrongdoing, and societal issues. This ability to report freely is essential for a functioning democracy, as it ensures transparency and promotes an informed electorate.

The First Amendment protects your right to speak, protest, and organize, allowing you to participate in the democratic process, challenge authority, and express your views. These rights ensure that the voices of individuals and groups are heard, providing a foundation for freedom of expression and political engagement in the United States.

Your Rights in Elections

Voting is one of the most fundamental rights and responsibilities in a democracy. The **U.S. Constitution** and its amendment's guarantee the right to vote to all eligible citizens, though this right has expanded over time through various amendments and laws to ensure greater inclusivity.

The Right to Vote (Fifteenth, Nineteenth, and Twenty-Sixth Amendments)

Several key amendments have expanded voting rights in the United States:

- **Fifteenth Amendment (1870)**: This amendment prohibits the denial of the right to vote based on **race, color, or previous condition of servitude**. It was a major step forward in ensuring that African American men, particularly in the Southern states, had the right to vote after the Civil War.

- **Nineteenth Amendment (1920)**: This amendment granted **women the right to vote**, marking a major victory for the women's suffrage movement.

- **Twenty-Sixth Amendment (1971)**: This amendment lowered the voting age to **18**, expanding the electorate to include young adults who had previously been excluded.

Voter Registration

In most states, you must be **registered** to vote, and each state has different registration rules. Some states allow same-day registration, while others require you to register weeks in advance of an election. Many states also offer online voter registration, and some offer automatic registration when you apply for a driver's license.

- **Voter ID Laws**: Some states require voters to show **identification** at the polls to verify their identity. The types of ID accepted and the rules around voter identification vary by state. While these laws are intended to prevent voter fraud, they have been criticized for disproportionately affecting minority, elderly, and low-income voters who may not have access to the required ID.

The Right to Equal Voting Power

The **One Person, One Vote** principle ensures that your vote carries equal weight in the election process. This principle has been reinforced by **Supreme Court rulings** that ensure districts are drawn in such a way that each person's vote has the same power, preventing any one vote from being overrepresented or underrepresented.

- **Gerrymandering**: Gerrymandering is the manipulation of electoral district boundaries to favor a particular political party or group. While gerrymandering is legal, it undermines the principle of equal representation. In recent years, courts and lawmakers have increasingly focused on how to prevent or address partisan gerrymandering.

Poll Taxes and Voter Suppression

While the **Twenty-Fourth Amendment (1964)** abolished **poll taxes** in federal elections, they had been used previously as a barrier to voting for poor African Americans and other marginalized groups. Despite this, other methods, such as **literacy tests, voter ID laws,** and **purging voter rolls**, continue to be used in some states to suppress voter participation, particularly among racial minorities.

- **Federal Oversight**: At times, the federal government has intervened in states with a history of voter discrimination. The **Voting Rights Act of 1965** was a major step in addressing these practices by requiring certain states with a history of discrimination to obtain federal approval before changing voting laws. However, parts of this act were struck down by the **Supreme Court** in 2013, leading to concerns about the continued protection of voting rights.

The Right to Secret Ballots

The **secret ballot** ensures that your vote is private and that you are not subject to coercion or intimidation when voting. The right to vote in private allows voters to express their true preferences without fear of retaliation or undue influence.

The Right to Fair and Free Elections

Elections must be **fair, free,** and conducted in a manner that reflects the will of the people. This includes:

- **Free Access to Polling Places**: Voting locations must be accessible to all eligible voters, regardless of their physical ability, geographic location, or socio-economic status.

- **Absentee and Early Voting**: Many states allow **early voting** or the ability to vote by **absentee ballot** for people who cannot make it to the polls on election day, such as military personnel, students, or individuals with disabilities.

Your rights in elections ensure that you can participate in the democratic process by casting your vote freely and without hindrance. The **right to vote**, **equal voting power**, **secret ballots**, and the elimination of barriers like poll taxes are key protections that uphold the integrity of U.S. democracy. These rights continue to be safeguarded and expanded as efforts to promote voter participation and prevent discrimination remain central to maintaining a fair electoral system.

What to Do When You Believe a Law Is Unconstitutional

If you believe that a law violates the Constitution, there are several steps you can take to challenge the law and protect your constitutional rights. The **U.S. Constitution** provides the framework for the legal process, ensuring that the government is bound by the limits it sets and that individuals can seek redress when their rights are violated.

Challenging a Law in Court

If you believe a law is unconstitutional, one of the most direct ways to challenge it is through the **court system**. Courts have the power to interpret laws and determine whether they align with the Constitution.

- **Filing a Lawsuit**: If you are directly affected by the law, you may be able to **file a lawsuit** in court challenging its constitutionality. For example, individuals who believe a law violates their **First Amendment rights** or **due process** protections might bring the case before a federal or state court.

- **Judicial Review**: The concept of **judicial review**— the power of courts to examine laws and determine whether they comply with the Constitution—was established in **Marbury v. Madison** (1803). If a court determines that a law is unconstitutional, it can **strike it down** or declare it invalid.

Using the Courts to Protect Your Rights

- **Legal Precedent**: Challenging a law often requires referencing **legal precedents**—past decisions in similar cases where courts have ruled on similar constitutional issues. Attorneys specializing in constitutional law can provide crucial insights into which cases can be used to support your argument.

- **Seeking Legal Representation**: Challenging the constitutionality of a law can be complex and may require expert legal counsel. If you are pursuing such a case, consider consulting an attorney who specializes in constitutional law or civil rights.

Advocating for Change

If you believe a law is unconstitutional, you can also work for change through **advocacy, lobbying**, or **petitioning the government**. Engaging with lawmakers, organizing public protests, or working with advocacy organizations can help bring attention to the issue and put pressure on elected officials to amend or repeal the law.

- **Petitioning the Government**: You have the right to **petition the government** under the **First Amendment**, and organizing petitions or campaigns can be a powerful tool for addressing perceived constitutional violations.

- **Public Advocacy**: Public advocacy through **social media, public forums**, or **legislative testimony** can help raise awareness of the issue and mobilize others to join the cause.

If you believe a law is unconstitutional, you can take steps to challenge it through the courts, work for change through advocacy, or petition the government for reform. The **judicial system**, particularly the power of **judicial review**, plays a crucial role in upholding the Constitution and ensuring that laws comply with the principles of justice and fairness.

Part VII: How the Constitution Is Interpreted

How Courts Decide Constitutional Cases

The process by which courts decide constitutional cases is essential for interpreting and applying the principles enshrined in the U.S. Constitution. Courts, particularly the **Supreme Court**, have the power to interpret the Constitution and resolve legal disputes based on constitutional principles. Understanding how courts approach constitutional cases can provide insight into how the law evolves over time and adapts to new societal issues.

Judicial Interpretation of the Constitution

Courts interpret the Constitution using various methods and approaches. These interpretations are shaped by judicial philosophy, legal principles, and the social context of the case. Courts consider the text of the Constitution, its historical context, and the evolving needs of society when making their decisions.

- **Textualism**: Textualism is an approach that focuses on the plain meaning of the text of the Constitution. Judges who follow this philosophy believe that the words of the Constitution should be interpreted as they were understood at the time they were written. Textualism emphasizes the importance of following the explicit language of the document.

- **Originalism**: Originalism is another common method of constitutional interpretation, which posits that the Constitution should be understood based on the **original intent** or **original meaning** of the framers. Originalists argue that the Constitution should be applied as it was intended by those who wrote it, and they look at the historical context and debates during the drafting of the Constitution to guide their interpretations.

- **Living Constitution**: The **Living Constitution** approach suggests that the Constitution should be interpreted in light of changing social, political, and economic conditions. Proponents of this view argue that the Constitution's principles must be applied flexibly, allowing the document to adapt to contemporary issues that the framers could not have anticipated.

Key Factors Courts Consider in Constitutional Cases

When deciding constitutional cases, courts consider several factors, including:

1. **Text of the Constitution**: The primary source for interpretation is the text itself. Courts examine the specific language of constitutional provisions, such as the **Bill of Rights** or other relevant articles, to determine how they apply to the case at hand.

2. **Historical Context**: Courts often look to the historical background of the Constitution and its amendments. Understanding the framers' intent or

the societal issues at the time can provide valuable context for interpreting certain provisions.

3. **Judicial Precedent**: Courts consider prior rulings on similar issues. **Precedent** helps ensure that the law is applied consistently over time and provides stability in legal interpretations.

4. **Principles of Justice**: Courts also consider principles of fairness, equality, and liberty. Constitutional interpretation often involves balancing competing interests, such as individual rights versus government power, or ensuring equal protection under the law.

Role of Lower Courts vs. Supreme Court

While lower courts hear constitutional cases and apply constitutional principles, the **Supreme Court** has the final say on interpreting the Constitution. The Court has the power to review cases brought before it, interpret the Constitution in light of new cases, and establish binding precedent.

- **Lower Courts**: Federal district courts and circuit courts hear cases involving constitutional issues, but their decisions can be appealed to higher courts. These courts often interpret the Constitution in light of Supreme Court rulings and may issue rulings that reflect evolving legal and societal norms.

- **Supreme Court**: As the highest court in the land, the Supreme Court has the final authority on constitutional interpretation. When the Court makes a ruling, it can reshape the law by either **upholding** or **striking down** laws that violate the Constitution.

The Impact of Constitutional Decisions

When courts rule on constitutional cases, their decisions can have a profound impact on the law and society. These decisions can set national precedents that affect everything from **civil rights** to **governmental powers** and **individual freedoms.**

For example, landmark decisions like **Brown v. Board of Education** (1954), which declared racial segregation in public schools unconstitutional, and **Roe v. Wade** (1973), which recognized a woman's right to choose an abortion, have significantly reshaped American society.

Courts decide constitutional cases through a complex process that involves interpreting the Constitution, considering historical context, examining legal precedents, and weighing the needs of society. The role of the courts, particularly the Supreme Court, is critical in ensuring that the Constitution is upheld and applied to the realities of modern life.

Judicial Review and Precedent

Judicial review and **precedent** are two key concepts that guide how courts interpret the Constitution and apply the law. These principles ensure that the judicial branch plays its crucial role in checking the powers of the legislative and executive branches while providing consistency and stability in the legal system.

Judicial Review

Judicial review is the power of the courts to review the constitutionality of laws, executive actions, and government policies. It allows the judiciary to invalidate laws or actions that conflict with the Constitution, ensuring that the government operates within its constitutional limits.

- **Origin of Judicial Review**: The principle of judicial review was established in the landmark **Supreme Court case Marbury v. Madison** (1803). In this case, Chief Justice **John Marshall** asserted that the courts had the authority to review acts of Congress and determine whether they were constitutional. Marshall famously wrote, "It is emphatically the province and duty of the judicial department to say what the law is."

- **Impact of Judicial Review**: Judicial review allows the courts to act as a **check** on the legislative and executive branches, ensuring that no branch exceeds its authority or infringes on individual rights. This power has been instrumental in cases that have shaped American law, including **Brown v. Board of Education** (racial segregation in public schools) and **Obergefell v. Hodges** (legalizing same-sex marriage).

- **Checks and Balances**: Judicial review is a vital component of the **checks and balances** system outlined in the Constitution. By granting the judiciary the power to strike down unconstitutional laws and executive actions, judicial review helps maintain the separation of powers between the branches of government.

Precedent (Stare Decisis)

Precedent refers to the principle of **stare decisis**, meaning "to stand by things decided." This legal doctrine dictates that courts should follow the rulings in previous cases when making decisions on similar legal issues. Precedent ensures stability, consistency, and predictability in the law.

- **Role of Precedent**: When a court makes a decision, that decision becomes **precedent** for future cases with similar facts or legal issues. Lower courts are generally required to follow the precedent set by higher courts, and the Supreme Court's decisions serve as the ultimate guide for the interpretation of constitutional principles.

- **Binding Precedent**: Binding precedent refers to legal principles set by a higher court that lower courts are obligated to follow. For example, decisions made by the U.S. Supreme Court are binding on all other courts in the country. If a lower court's decision contradicts a Supreme Court ruling, the Supreme Court's interpretation will prevail.

- **Stare Decisis and Flexibility**: While stare decisis encourages consistency in the law, it does not prevent the courts from overturning precedent if circumstances change or if a previous decision is deemed unjust. The **Supreme Court** has, at times, overturned precedent to reflect evolving societal values or new legal understandings. For example, the Supreme Court reversed its decision in **Plessy v. Ferguson** (1896) with **Brown v. Board of Education** (1954), declaring that racial segregation in public schools was unconstitutional.

Judicial Review and Precedent in Action

The combination of **judicial review** and **precedent** allows courts to maintain the integrity of the Constitution while adapting the law to changing circumstances. These concepts play out in cases such as:

- **Roe v. Wade (1973)**: The Supreme Court's decision that legalized abortion relied heavily on **precedent** and the constitutional right to privacy, a principle rooted in earlier rulings like **Griswold v. Connecticut** (1965). The Court exercised **judicial review** to assess the constitutionality of state laws regulating abortion and struck down many state restrictions as unconstitutional.

- **Obergefell v. Hodges (2015)**: The Supreme Court used **judicial review** to determine that same-sex marriage bans were unconstitutional, building on

precedent related to marriage equality, individual rights, and privacy. The Court cited evolving standards of equality and justice to extend marriage rights to same-sex couples.

Judicial review and **precedent** are integral to the American legal system, ensuring that the Constitution is upheld, and that the law evolves in response to new challenges. Judicial review empowers the courts to act as a check on the other branches of government, while precedent ensures that the law remains consistent and predictable. Together, these principles maintain the integrity of the judicial process and safeguard the rights of individuals in an ever-changing society.

Federal Power vs. State Power

The balance of power between the **federal government** and the **state governments** is one of the most fundamental principles in American constitutional law. This concept, known as **federalism**, ensures that power is divided and shared between two levels of government to prevent any one entity from becoming too powerful. The tension between federal and state power has been a central theme in American history and continues to shape the country's legal and political landscape.

The Constitution and Federalism

The **U.S. Constitution** creates a system of **dual sovereignty**, where both the federal government and the states have distinct areas of authority. The Constitution outlines the powers of the federal government and leaves all other powers to the states or the people.

- **Enumerated Powers of the Federal Government**: The **federal government** is granted specific powers under the Constitution, primarily in **Article I, Section 8**, where **enumerated powers** are listed. These powers include the ability to regulate interstate commerce, coin money, declare war, raise and support armed forces, and conduct foreign affairs. These powers allow the federal government to address national concerns that transcend state borders, such as national defense, foreign policy, and interstate trade.

- **Reserved Powers of the States**: The **Tenth Amendment** reinforces the idea of state sovereignty by stating that any powers not specifically granted to the federal government, nor prohibited to the states by the Constitution, are **reserved to the states or the people**. This allows states to regulate areas such as education, law enforcement, public health, and local commerce. States have the ability to govern their own internal affairs, provided they do not conflict with federal laws.

- **Concurrent Powers**: Both the federal government and the states share certain powers, known as **concurrent powers**. These include the power to tax, the power to enforce laws, and the power to establish courts. These shared powers reflect the practical need for cooperation between the two levels of government in certain areas.

Supremacy Clause and Federal Authority

The **Supremacy Clause** (Article VI, Clause 2) of the Constitution asserts that **federal law** takes precedence over state law. It states:

"This Constitution, and the Laws of the United States which shall be made in Pursuance thereof; and all Treaties made, or which shall be made, under the Authority of the United States, shall be the supreme Law of the Land; and the Judges in every State shall be bound thereby, any Thing in the Constitution or Laws of any State to the Contrary notwithstanding."

- **Federal Precedence**: When a state law conflicts with federal law, **federal law prevails**. This ensures a uniform legal framework across the nation, especially in areas like civil rights, immigration, and interstate commerce. For example, federal civil rights laws mandate equal treatment, which supersedes state laws that might allow discrimination.

- **McCulloch v. Maryland (1819)**: A landmark case that reinforced federal power, the Supreme Court ruled that the federal government could exercise powers not explicitly stated in the Constitution through the **Necessary and Proper Clause** (also known as the **Elastic Clause**). The case also held that states cannot tax federal institutions, affirming the principle of **federal supremacy**.

The Evolution of Federal vs. State Power

The balance between federal and state power has shifted over time due to societal changes, judicial rulings, and political movements.

- **New Deal Era**: During the **New Deal** in the 1930s, President Franklin D. Roosevelt implemented a series of federal programs to address the Great Depression. The federal government's role expanded significantly during this time, particularly in areas of economic regulation, social welfare, and labor rights. The **Supreme Court** upheld many of these initiatives, expanding the reach of federal power.

- **Civil Rights Movement**: In the 1960s, the federal government played a significant role in enforcing civil rights protections, overriding state laws that allowed racial segregation and discrimination. Landmark cases like **Brown v. Board of Education (1954)** and **civil rights legislation** passed by Congress were critical in ensuring national standards for equality and justice.

- **Recent Trends**: In recent decades, there has been a push for greater state sovereignty, with states challenging federal authority on issues like healthcare, environmental regulations, and immigration policy. The ongoing debate about the scope of federal power versus state power is exemplified by cases like **NFIB v. Sebelius (2012)**, which upheld the individual mandate in the Affordable Care Act (ACA) while limiting the federal government's ability to force states to expand Medicaid.

Key Areas of Tension Between Federal and State Power

Several issues remain sources of tension between federal and state governments:

- **Healthcare**: The **Affordable Care Act (ACA)** was a significant expansion of federal authority, requiring individuals to obtain health insurance or face a penalty. Some states have challenged the law, arguing that it infringes on state sovereignty and individual freedom.

- **Immigration**: While immigration is primarily a federal issue, states have often passed their own laws regarding immigration enforcement, leading to conflicts between state and federal policies. For example, states like **Arizona** have attempted to enforce their own immigration laws, sometimes clashing with federal immigration policies.

- **Marijuana Legalization**: Several states have legalized marijuana for medical or recreational use, even though federal law continues to classify marijuana as an illegal substance. This creates an ongoing conflict between state and federal law enforcement, with some states seeking greater autonomy in regulating the use of marijuana.

The relationship between federal and state power is dynamic, evolving with societal changes and political challenges. While the Constitution provides a framework for shared powers, the balance between federal authority and state sovereignty continues to be a central issue in American governance. Through **judicial review**, **legal precedent**, and **political action**, the courts and lawmakers work to define the limits and scope of each level of government's power.

Common Myths and Misunderstandings About the Constitution

The U.S. Constitution is often hailed as one of the most important legal documents in history, but despite its foundational role in American governance, there are several myths and misconceptions about its contents and application. Understanding these myths is crucial for properly interpreting the Constitution and the rights it guarantees.

Myth #1: The Constitution Guarantees Absolute Freedom of Speech

While the **First Amendment** guarantees the **freedom of speech**, it does not provide absolute protection for all types of speech. Certain categories of speech are not protected by the First Amendment, including:

- **Incitement to Violence**: Speech that incites imminent lawless action is not protected (e.g., shouting "fire" in a crowded theater when there is no fire).

- **Defamation**: **Libel** (written defamation) and **slander** (spoken defamation) are not protected forms of speech if they harm someone's reputation.

- **Hate Speech**: While hate speech is generally protected, speech that directly incites violence or hatred against specific groups can be subject to regulation.

Myth #2: The Bill of Rights Applies Only to the Federal Government

A common misunderstanding is that the **Bill of Rights** (the first ten amendments to the Constitution) applies only to the federal government. In reality, over time, the protections in the Bill of Rights have been **incorporated** to apply to the states through the **Fourteenth Amendment's Due Process Clause**.

- **Selective Incorporation**: Through Supreme Court decisions, many rights guaranteed in the Bill of Rights, such as **freedom of speech** and **freedom of the press**, have been extended to state governments. However, not all provisions of the Bill of Rights have been incorporated—some are still only applicable at the federal level.

Myth #3: The Constitution Requires a Supermajority to Amend

A common myth is that the Constitution requires a **supermajority** for any amendment to pass. In fact, while amending the Constitution requires a higher level of approval, the process is not as difficult as some may think.

- **Amendment Process**: The Constitution can be amended in two ways:
  1. **Congress** can propose an amendment with a two-thirds vote in both the **House of Representatives** and the **Senate**.
  2. **A constitutional convention** can be called by **two-thirds of state legislatures**.

After an amendment is proposed, it must be ratified by **three-fourths of state legislatures** or by conventions in **three-fourths of the states**. While this is a high threshold, it does not require a supermajority of the population, only the states or legislatures.

Myth #4: The Constitution Created a Direct Democracy

Many believe that the **U.S. Constitution** established a direct democracy, where citizens vote on every law or policy directly. However, the **Constitution** established a **representative democracy**.

- **Representative Democracy**: The Constitution creates a system where citizens vote for **representatives** (such as members of Congress, governors, and presidents) who then make decisions on their behalf. This is in contrast to a direct democracy, where citizens vote on every issue directly.

Myth #5: The Constitution is a Fixed Document

Some people believe that the Constitution is a static document that cannot change, but in reality, it is a **living document** that has evolved over time.

- **Living Constitution**: The Constitution was designed to be flexible and adaptable to changing circumstances. Through **judicial interpretation, amendments**, and **legislation**, the Constitution has been interpreted to reflect new challenges and societal developments, from **civil rights** to **technology**.

Myth #6: The Founders Agreed on Every Aspect of the Constitution

There is a misconception that the **Founding Fathers** were in complete agreement about the Constitution's provisions. In truth, the drafting of the Constitution involved significant debate and compromise.

- **Debates and Compromises**: Issues such as the **structure of government, representation**, and the **role of the executive branch** were hotly debated during the Constitutional Convention. For example, the **Great Compromise** established a bicameral legislature, balancing the interests of large and small states.

While the U.S. Constitution is a foundational document in American governance, many myths and misunderstandings surround it. By correcting these misconceptions, we gain a clearer understanding of how the Constitution works, the rights it guarantees, and the principles it upholds. Understanding the Constitution is key to understanding American democracy and the protections it offers to all citizens.

Part VIII: Reference and Tools

A Short Timeline of Constitutional Change

This timeline highlights key moments in the history of the U.S. Constitution and its amendments, showing how the document has evolved to meet the changing needs of the nation. From the founding of the country to the latest amendments, the Constitution has been amended and interpreted to reflect evolving societal values and challenges.

1787: Constitutional Convention and the U.S. Constitution

- **May 25 - September 17, 1787**: The **Constitutional Convention** convenes in Philadelphia with the goal of revising the Articles of Confederation, which had proven ineffective in governing the newly independent states. The delegates ultimately decide to create a new framework for government, resulting in the drafting of the **U.S. Constitution**.

1789: Ratification of the Constitution

- **March 4, 1789**: The **U.S. Constitution** officially goes into effect after being ratified by enough states, replacing the Articles of Confederation. George Washington is elected as the first President of the United States.

- September 25, 1789: The **Bill of Rights** is proposed to address concerns about individual liberties and to secure support for the Constitution.

1791: The Bill of Rights

- December 15, 1791: The **Bill of Rights**, the first ten amendments to the Constitution, is ratified. These amendments guarantee essential freedoms such as the **freedom of speech, religion, assembly, bearing arms**, and protections against **unreasonable searches and seizures.**

1861-1865: The Civil War

- The **Civil War** (1861-1865) results in the preservation of the Union and ends the institution of **slavery** in the United States.

1865: The Thirteenth Amendment

- December 6, 1865: The **Thirteenth Amendment** is ratified, abolishing slavery and involuntary servitude in the United States.

1868: The Fourteenth Amendment

- July 9, 1868: The **Fourteenth Amendment** is ratified, granting **citizenship** to all persons born or naturalized in the United States and guaranteeing **equal protection under the law**. This amendment is critical in the fight for civil rights.

1870: The Fifteenth Amendment

- **February 3, 1870**: The Fifteenth Amendment is ratified, prohibiting the denial of voting rights based on race, color, or previous condition of servitude, giving African American men the right to vote.

1920: The Nineteenth Amendment

- **August 18, 1920**: The Nineteenth Amendment is ratified, granting women the right to vote. This marks the culmination of the **women's suffrage movement**, a decades-long struggle for women's voting rights.

1964: The Twenty-Fourth Amendment

- **January 23, 1964**: The Twenty-Fourth Amendment is ratified, eliminating poll taxes in federal elections. Poll taxes were used to disenfranchise poor and minority voters, especially in the South.

1965: The Voting Rights Act

- **August 6, 1965**: The Voting Rights Act is signed into law, outlawing discriminatory practices such as literacy tests and poll taxes, and ensuring federal oversight of elections in areas with a history of discrimination.

1971: The Twenty-Sixth Amendment

- **July 1, 1971**: The Twenty-Sixth Amendment is ratified, lowering the voting age from 21 to 18, a response to the argument that if 18-year-olds were old enough to be drafted into the military, they should also be allowed to vote.

2013: Shelby County v. Holder

- The **Supreme Court** rules in **Shelby County v. Holder** (2013) that key parts of the **Voting Rights Act** are unconstitutional, specifically the formula used to determine which states required federal approval for changes to voting laws. This decision significantly affects voting rights protections.

Ongoing Debates

- The Constitution continues to evolve in response to social, political, and technological changes, with ongoing debates about issues such as **immigration, marriage equality, healthcare**, and **gun rights**.

Landmark Supreme Court Cases (Brief Summaries)

Over the years, the U.S. **Supreme Court** has issued landmark rulings that have shaped the interpretation of the Constitution. These cases address critical issues such as **civil rights**, **government powers**, and the balance between individual liberties and state authority.

Marbury v. Madison (1803)

- **Issue**: Established the principle of **judicial review**, the power of the courts to review and potentially invalidate laws that violate the Constitution.

- **Outcome**: The Supreme Court, led by **Chief Justice John Marshall**, declared a portion of the Judiciary Act of 1789 unconstitutional, establishing the judiciary's role in interpreting the Constitution and asserting its authority to check the actions of the other branches.

Brown v. Board of Education (1954)

- **Issue**: Whether state-sponsored racial segregation in public schools violated the **Equal Protection Clause** of the **Fourteenth Amendment**.

- **Outcome**: The Court ruled that racial segregation in public schools was inherently unequal and unconstitutional, overturning the precedent set by **Plessy v. Ferguson** (1896). This decision was pivotal in the **Civil Rights Movement** and led to the desegregation of schools.

Roe v. Wade (1973)

- **Issue**: Whether a state law banning abortions except to save the life of the mother was unconstitutional under a woman's **right to privacy**.

- **Outcome**: The Supreme Court recognized a woman's **constitutional right** to choose to have an abortion under the **right to privacy** implied by the **Due Process Clause** of the **Fourteenth Amendment**, thereby legalizing abortion across the United States.

Miranda v. Arizona (1966)

- **Issue**: Whether the Fifth Amendment's protection against self-incrimination extends to police interrogation.

- **Outcome**: The Court ruled that criminal suspects must be informed of their rights to remain silent and to an attorney when arrested (the **Miranda warning**). This decision fundamentally changed law enforcement practices across the country.

Obergefell v. Hodges (2015)

- **Issue**: Whether the **Fourteenth Amendment** requires all states to grant and recognize same-sex marriage.

- **Outcome**: The Court ruled that **same-sex marriage** is a constitutional right, requiring all states to recognize and perform such marriages, marking a significant victory for the **LGBTQ+** **rights** movement.

Glossary of Constitutional Terms

This glossary provides definitions of essential terms used in constitutional law and practice, helping to clarify the legal language and concepts that underpin the U.S. Constitution.

Amendment

- A formal change or addition to the Constitution. The Constitution has been amended 27 times since its ratification in 1789.

Bill of Rights

- The first ten amendments to the U.S. Constitution, which guarantee fundamental rights such as freedom of speech, freedom of religion, and the right to a fair trial.

Checks and Balances

- A system in which each branch of government (executive, legislative, and judicial) has some measure of influence over the other branches to prevent any one branch from gaining too much power.

Federalism

- The division of power between the federal government and the state governments. It allows both levels of government to have authority over certain areas, while the Constitution defines the scope of federal and state powers.

Judicial Review

- The power of the courts to review and potentially invalidate laws and actions of the other branches of government if they are found to be unconstitutional.

Sovereignty

- The authority of a state to govern itself and make its own laws without interference from external forces.

Stare Decisis

- The principle that courts should follow established precedent when making decisions in similar cases. This ensures consistency and predictability in the law.

Frequently Asked Questions

This section answers common questions people have about the Constitution and its application in everyday life.

Q: Can the Constitution be changed?

- Yes, the Constitution can be amended. The process requires approval by two-thirds of both **houses of Congress** and ratification by three-fourths of state legislatures. This process has been used to make 27 amendments, including significant ones like the **Bill of Rights**, the **Abolition of Slavery**, and the **Extension of Voting Rights**.

Q: What is the Bill of Rights?

- The **Bill of Rights** refers to the first ten amendments to the U.S. Constitution. These amendments guarantee a range of personal freedoms, such as freedom of speech, the right to bear arms, and protection from unreasonable searches and seizures.

Q: Does the Constitution give everyone the right to vote?

- While the Constitution has expanded voting rights over time through several amendments (including the **Fifteenth, Nineteenth, and Twenty-Sixth Amendments**), **voting rights** have been further defined by federal and state laws, and **voter eligibility** can still be limited by factors such as age, criminal history, and residency.

Q: Can the President change the Constitution?

- No, the President cannot unilaterally change the Constitution. Amendments must be proposed by Congress or through a constitutional convention and ratified by the states. However, the President plays a key role in shaping public policy and interpreting the Constitution.

Study and Discussion Questions

These questions are designed to encourage deeper reflection and discussion about the Constitution, its principles, and its impact on American life.

1. How does the system of checks and balances help protect against abuses of power in the government?

  • Discuss the ways in which the separation of powers between the three branches of government ensures that no single branch becomes too powerful. Consider real-world examples such as **vetoes**, **judicial review**, and **Senate confirmations**.

2. How have the interpretations of the First Amendment evolved over time, particularly regarding freedom of speech and religion?

  • Explore key court cases such as **Schenck v. United States** (1919) and **Engel v. Vitale** (1962) to understand how the interpretation of **freedom of speech** and **freedom of religion** has shifted with societal changes.

3. In what ways have the Thirteenth, Fourteenth, and Fifteenth Amendments changed the political and social landscape of the United States?

  • Examine the historical context of these amendments, particularly in relation to the abolition of slavery and the fight for civil rights. How have these amendments impacted legal cases related to equality and justice?

4. What challenges does the Constitution face in the modern age, especially in light of technological advancements and social changes?

- Discuss contemporary issues like **digital privacy, social media regulation,** and **voting rights.** How do the **principles** of the Constitution continue to provide guidance, and where might new interpretations or amendments be necessary?

As we reach the end of this journey through the U.S. Constitution, it is clear that this living document remains as vital today as it was when it was first written over two centuries ago. The Constitution not only provides the framework for our government but also ensures the protection of the rights and freedoms that form the foundation of American democracy. From the **Bill of Rights** to the ongoing debates about federalism, individual rights, and equality, the Constitution continues to evolve, shaping the course of our nation.

By understanding the principles and values embedded within the Constitution, we empower ourselves to engage more meaningfully in the democratic process. Whether it's exercising our right to vote, challenging unconstitutional laws, or standing up for justice, the Constitution provides the tools for every citizen to participate in and protect the liberties we hold dear.

The journey of interpreting, living, and upholding the Constitution is ongoing. As society changes and new challenges emerge, we must continue to reflect on its principles and ensure that they remain true to the vision of liberty, equality, and justice for all.

Thank you for taking the time to explore this essential document. May this understanding inspire you to become an active and informed participant in shaping the future of this nation, just as the Constitution's framers intended. The Constitution is not just a document of the past; it is a living testament to the enduring ideals that continue to guide us toward a more perfect union.

The journey doesn't end here. It is, in fact, just the beginning.

www.ingramcontent.com/pod-product-compliance
Lightning Source LLC
Chambersburg PA
CBHW072238270326
41930CB00010B/2185